BEGINNER'S

SHONA

(CHISHONA)

HIPPOCRENE BEGINNER'S SERIES

Arabic
Armenian
Assyrian
Basque
Bulgarian
Chinese
Czech
Dutch
French
Gaelic
Hungarian
Irish
Italian
Japanese
Lithuanian
Maori
Persian
Polish
Romanian
Russian
Serbo-Croatian
Shona
Sicilian
Slovak
Spanish (Latin American)
Swedish
Turkish
Ukrainian
Vietnamese
Welsh

BEGINNER'S
SHONA
(CHISHONA)

Aquilina Mawadza

HIPPOCRENE BOOKS
New York

© 2003 Aquilina Mawadza

ISBN 0-7818-0864-2

For information, address:
    Hippocrene Books, Inc.
    171 Madison Avenue
    New York, NY 10016

Cataloging in Publication data available from the Library of Congress.

Printed in the United States of America.

CONTENTS

ACKNOWLEDGMENTS

This book could not have been completed without the help of many people. I would like to thank the editors, Caroline Gates and Anne Kemper, and my husband Crispen Mawadza for their advice and comments while writing this book. Many thanks also go to friends and colleagues, and Pedzisai Mashiri, Katrina Thompson, and Owen Robinson who contributed their thoughts and ideas. Finally thanks to Hippocrene Books for giving me the opportunity to publish *Beginner's Shona.*

INTRODUCTION

This book is designed for travelers and students, who will find it useful in gaining an understanding of the Shona language and culture. It assumes little or no previous knowledge of the Shona language, and focuses on general, but socially useful, conversations that are explored through dialogues. The student will be introduced to various aspects of Shona grammar as well as cultural facts, and will be given a working proficiency in the Shona language so as to satisfy social demands as well as business needs.

The book is composed of two sections. The first section consists of information about Zimbabwe, where Shona is the national language: geography, climate, population, history, economy, religion, culture and the arts, hints about everyday living, shopping, driving, health, and much more. The second section is designed to teach the beginning student the basics of the language and to provide the means for general communication in Shona. The lessons consist of practice dialogues, topics of grammar, and review exercises. Each dialogue is presented in Shona and English side-by-side, followed by a list of the vocabulary and essential expressions presented, also with their English translations. You will learn useful phrases and words for special situations. Basic grammar is introduced in each lesson, teaching the structure and fundamental constructions of the Shona language. Although the lessons cannot cover all of the grammatical concepts, they will teach you enough to feel comfortable speaking in a variety of situations that are described herein, and will provide an essential base for future study. With this small and compact book, you will be able to carry out satisfying conversations in Shona.

ZIMBABWE

GEOGRAPHY, CLIMATE, AND POPULATION

Geography

Zimbabwe is a landlocked country in southern Africa, covering a total area of 390,580 square kilometers. It is surrounded by Zambia in the north, South Africa in the south, Mozambique in the east and Botswana in the southwest.

Zimbabwe consists mostly of open grasslands, lying between 900 to 1700 meters above sea level. It is located between two of Africa's greatest rivers, the Zambezi in the northwest and the Limpopo in the southeast. The Eastern Highlands form Zimbabwe's mountainous region with a range that stretches from the Nyanga region in the north to the Chimanimani Mountains in the south.

Climate

Zimbabwe has a relatively temperate climate. The winters stretch from May to August and can be compared to summers that are experienced in the Mediterranean, with cool, clear nights and warm sunny days. On the plateau, freezing temperatures and overnight frosts are common.

In the lower-lying areas, hot and humid conditions are experienced. The country's rainy season is in the summer months, from November to April. During the summer, temperatures are rarely below thirty degrees Celsius. The winter months are the most comfortable for traveling.

Population

The population of Zimbabwe is estimated to be 11.7 million (Inter-Censal Demographic Survey Report, 1997:19) with an annual growth rate of 3 percent since 1985.

The majority of the population is settled in the rural areas. The Shona group constitutes about 76 percent of the population and occupies the eastern two-thirds of the country. The Ndebele are settled mainly in the southwestern region and account for 18 percent of the population. The rest of the population is divided between minority groups that include the Tonga, Kalanga, Shangani, Venda, Chewa, Nambya, Asians and Europeans. The major cities are Harare, Bulawayo, Gweru, Mutare and Masvingo. Harare is the largest city with a population of 1.5 million.

HISTORY

There has been a variety of civilizations in Zimbabwe as shown by the ancient stone structures at Khami, Great Zimbabwe and Dhlo-Dhlo. The Mutapa was the first major civilization to become established in the region. In the 1490s, King Mutota's empire included almost all of the present-day Zimbabwe plateau and parts of what is now Mozambique (Beach 198). The wealth of the Mutapa empire was based on small-scale industries, such as iron smelting and agriculture. Trade was conducted with Arab and Swahili merchants. The Portuguese came in the early sixteenth century, destroyed this trade, and began a series of wars. This led to the decline of the empire in the seventeenth century. In the seventeenth century, after the collapse of the Mutapa empire, a number of Shona states came together and formed the Rozvi empire, which covered more than half of present-day Zimbabwe. By 1690, the Portuguese had been driven out and the land formerly under the Mutapa was controlled by the Rozvi. By 1840, a new militant dynasty, the Zulu, led by Shaka, emerged from the south. They conquered the Rozvi dynasty but never succeeded in subjugating the Rozvi.

Tales from the African continent made their way to England through missionaries like Robert Moffat. The "discovery" of Victoria Falls by David Livingstone increased the curiosity of young people who were in search of adventure. The arrival of Cecil John Rhodes in 1890 secured Zimbabwe as a British colony, which immediately became known as Rhodesia outside of Africa. The British settlers prospered despite continued uprisings and revolts, such as the first Chimurenga war of liberation, led by two spirit mediums, Mbuya Nehanda and Sekuru Kaguvi, in 1896. The British continued to rule for the next eighty-five years.

In 1957, the Southern Rhodesian African National Congress, led by Joshua Nkomo, spearheaded the struggle for independence. In 1963, the nationalists split and the Zimbabwe African People's Union (ZAPU) was formed, and led by Joshua Nkomo. The Zimbabwe African National Union (ZANU) was formed under the leadership of Robert Mugabe. Ian Smith, who had become prime minister in 1964, began pushing for independence from Britain. When he found Britain's conditions for granting independence unacceptable to the country's white population, he unilaterally declared independence on November 11, 1965.

Free and fair elections were held in 1980 and ZANU came into power under the leadership of Robert Mugabe. In 1987, constitutional changes came into place whereby Robert Mugabe became executive president. In the same year, the Unity Accord brought about unification of the two major political parties, ZANU and ZAPU. The Movement for Democratic Change (MDC) was formed in 2000 and became the official opposition party after the 2000 parliamentary elections. Zimbabwe is now a multiparty parliamentary democracy.

ECONOMY

The majority of the Zimbabwean population is dependent on agriculture. The staple food crop is maize, with cotton, coffee, tea, sugarcane and grapes as the primary cash crops. Tobacco is Zimbabwe's largest export earner. The country also supplies fresh flowers, vegetables and citrus fruits to the European market. Other agricultural products include cattle, sheep, pigs, peanuts and wheat.

Mining constitutes 40 percent of the exports. This includes gold, coal, iron ore, copper, asbestos, chrome, nickel and tin.

Textiles dominate the manufacturing industry and, after South Africa, Zimbabwe offers the largest range of products in sub-Saharan Africa.

Developing industries include forestry and tourism. Major sectors of the economy consist of agriculture (28%), industry (32%), and services (40%).

ARTS AND CULTURE

Rock art that was created by the area's original inhabitants, the San, is scattered throughout the country. The San used fine brushes and a mixture of crushed iron ore, plant matter and animal fat to paint rock surfaces.

Many talented artists in Zimbabwe make a living from their art, and the country's stone sculptures have gained international recognition. The sculptures constitute a major collection in the National Gallery in Harare, which presents a wide range of displays, from early African art to colonial and postcolonial painting and sculpture. Chapungu Sculpture Park in Harare is also a place worth visiting for examples of this art form.

There exist many other monuments and sights of interest. The National Archives in Harare carries a collection of historic books and documents dating back to the sixteenth century. The Heroes Acre in Harare is a shrine to the liberation struggle and the heroes of the liberation war are buried there. The Museum of National History covers topics ranging from botany and geology to history.

The ruins of Great Zimbabwe together with Victoria Falls constitute the country's greatest attractions. A religious and secular capital with a population of 10,000 to 20,000 people, Great Zimbabwe was the greatest medieval city in sub-Saharan Africa. Between the thirteenth and fifteenth centuries the people of Great Zimbabwe controlled an area that stretched from across eastern Zimbabwe into Botswana, Mozambique and South Africa. The monument is in southeastern Zimbabwe. Victoria Falls is one of the world's most spectacular sites. Located on the Zambezi River and the Zimbabwe/Zambia border, the falls measure 1.7 kilometers (1 mile) wide and drop between 90 and 107 meters (300–350 feet) into the Zambezi Gorge.

RELIGION

The dominant religion practiced by the people of Zimbabwe is characterized by a mixture of Christianity and African traditional religion. While 40–50 percent of Zimbabweans belong to Christian churches, most believe in a hybrid of Christian and traditional beliefs. The Mwari cult is the major non-Christian religion, and in Shona, the Christian God is known as Mwari. Dating back to the 1300s, the Mwari cult was probably brought into Zimbabwe by migrating Bantu herders. The Mwari cult is a monotheistic belief that involves ancestor worship. Mwari, the Supreme Being, speaks to humans through an oracle.

In the urban areas, there are small Jewish, Muslim and Hindu communities.

ENTERTAINMENT, MUSIC, AND SPORTS

Live musical shows and discos are offered in bars and nightclubs in and around the city. The entertainment section of a newspaper is the best guide to find out who is performing and where. Zimbabwe's major towns have movie theaters, usually dominated by American action movies. Other forms of entertainment are rural fairs, school theater productions and traditional weddings.

Zimbabwe has a rich musical heritage and music plays an important cultural role. Present-day music in Zimbabwe, as in early oral society, reveals information about people's lives and past experiences. The most celebrated musicians include Thomas Mapfumo with his *chimurenga* "revolutionary" music, Oliver Mutukudzi, Simon Chimbetu, Stella Chiweshe and Leonard Zhakata.

Shona music is predominantly based on the *mbira*, a thumb piano. Thomas Mapfumo, for example, is one of Zimbabwe's singers who have successfully translated mbira music into a modern context.

The mbira pervades all aspects of Shona culture and is used to contact deceased ancestors at all-night ceremonies known as *bira*. It is believed that at the bira, the ancestral spirits, *vadzimu*, give guidance on family as well as community matters. Playing mbira is required to bring rain in times of drought and to stop rain during floods. It is also used as an instrument to chase away evil and harmful spirits, as well as to cure illnesses.

Another traditional musical instrument is the *marimba* (xylophone). Its keys are made from hardwood while the sound boxes are made of dry gourds. The *ngoma* (drum) is another traditional instrument and is made from cowhide and specially selected tree trunks, depending on the size and shape of the drum.

Musical styles from South Africa are popular because of its proximity. *Rumba* is another African style from Zaire that has become popular in Zimbabwe. Contemporary music from the western world is also quite popular with the young generation, such as R & B, hip-hop, and rock.

Every town has a public swimming pool, as well as golf courses and tennis courts. Fishing is possible in the many small artificial lakes in the national parks. There are also exciting fishing parks as well as resorts along Lake Kariba and the Zambezi River. Whitewater rafting and bungee jumping is possible on Victoria Falls. Mountain climbing, with rock climbs of ranging difficulty, can be done in the eastern highlands, the mountainous region of the country.

EVERYDAY LIFE

Forms of Address

There are two ways of addressing people in the Shona language: formally and informally. You may greet or address a younger person in an informal way by saying *Kanjani?, Uri bhoo?* (to mean "hi" and "how are you?" respectively). If the person is older or if you do not really know the person well, then the formal term of address is used, e.g. *Maswera sei?* (How did you spend the day?) and *Makadini?* (How are you?) For men, the prefix *Va-* is used to denote respect, e.g. *VaMakunde* "Mr. Makunde." For women, the respectful term is *Amai* or *Mai*, e.g. *Amai Makunde* "Mrs. Makunde."

Customs and Courtesies

When learning the Shona language, it is vital to realize the importance of respect for elder people. The plural forms of respect are used when addressing older people. Elders may also be addressed using their second names or the names of their children.

In greeting, one must spend time asking about the welfare of other family members. A handshake accompanies greetings and, while greeting someone and at other various times, one supports one's right hand with the left hand as a sign of respect. When two people greet each other, the person who greets first must wait for the response. Women and girls usually curtsy with bent knees when greeting, and when offering or receiving something.

The totem is an important symbol of identity for the Shona people. A totem is usually an animal's name, for instance *shumba* (lion). Addressing a person by their totem is highly respectful and very formal, especially in rural communities.

Hands are clapped during greetings, before and after eating, as well as upon receiving a gift. Men clap their hands with the palms and fingers together while women clap with one hand across the other.

City Transportation

Most of the big cities have good transportation systems. Harare's system includes buses, omnibuses and taxis. Taxis are also available in the smaller towns.

Taxi

Harare's taxi service operates twenty-four hours a day. There are taxi stands at the airport, train stations and in the town center. You also can stop a taxi anywhere by waving your hand.

Bus

You can get to almost any place in Zimbabwe by taking a bus. You do not need to reserve a seat in advance, unless you are traveling on the luxury coaches.

Driving, Car Rentals, and Traffic Rules

Zimbabwe has a good central network of tarred roads. Minor roads, however, are not usually tarred and can sometimes be difficult to drive.

Three basic kinds of gas are available: blend, unleaded and diesel.

The major tourist sites can be reached in a standard rental car. The main car rental companies are Hertz, Avis and Europcar. Driving is on the left as in the United Kingdom. Most road signs are internationally recognized and therefore easy to follow. The speed limit on Zimbabwean roads is 120 km/hour for vehicles on highways and 80 km/hour for buses. City limits are also specified accordingly. (See the Highway Code, Ministry of Transport.) It is advisable to avoid driving at night, especially in the rural areas, as goats, cattle and livestock may cross the road without warning.

Currency

One Zimbabwean Dollar (ZWD) is equal to 100 cents. Bills are available in denominations of ZWD 10,00, 20,00, 50,00, 100,00, and 500,00. Coins are available in ZWD 1, 5, 10, 20, 50, 1,00, 2,00, and 5,00. (The comma is used instead of a decimal point.)

Shopping

Food stores are open from 8:00 AM to approximately 6:00 PM during weekdays and until 1:00 PM on Saturdays. Most of these stores are closed on Sundays, but some stores stay open at the big shopping malls. Supermarkets and small service stores are common. You will also find small specialty stores for meat, baked foods, fruits and vegetables, and dairy products.

Department stores are open from 8:00 AM to about 6:00 PM during weekdays and until 1:00 PM on Saturdays. Most department stores are closed on Sundays too.

Zimbabwe offers a good selection of clothes and fabric made from natural fibers and decorated with various designs ranging from hand-painted batiks to tie-dye patterns. Art works can be found at sculpture parks throughout Zimbabwe. Crafts such as baskets and pottery can be found at markets and curio shops.

Festivals

Festivals on Zimbabwe's calendar:

Date	Holiday / Event
April 18	Independence Day
Late April/early May	Zimbabwe International Trade Fair
May 25	Africa Day
Late July/early August	Zimbabwe International Book Fair
August 11 and 12	Heroes' Day and Defense Forces' Day
End of August	Harare Agricultural Show
Early December	National Tree Planting Day
December 22	Unity Accord

Time

Zimbabwe is two hours ahead of Greenwich Mean Time (GMT), one hour ahead of European Winter Time, seven hours ahead of U.S. Eastern Standard Time and approximately eight hours behind Australia.

Communications

In spite of the long lines at the post office, especially in Harare, the postal system is reasonably efficient. Airmail takes about a week to Europe and about a week and a half to the Americas. The cheapest freight service for shipping goods is the Zimbabwean national cargo airline Affretair.

There are plenty of telephone facilities in the major cities. Local calls are relatively cheap and reasonably efficient. Phone cards can be bought from the post office. It is easy to dial directly to almost any part of the world. The international access code is 00 then 44 for the U.K., 1 for the U.S. and Canada, 27 for South Africa and 61 for Australia.

Facilities to send and receive faxes are also available, and Internet cafés can be found in the major cities.

Media

There are a number of English newspapers. These include *The Herald, The Sunday Mail, The Chronicle, The Financial Gazette, The Daily News, The Zimbabwe Standard,* and *The Zimbabwe Independent. Kwayedza* is a weekly newspaper in Shona.

There are four radio stations in Zimbabwe. Radio Two broadcasts in Shona and the other three stations broadcast mainly in English. BBC World and CNN can also be heard in Zimbabwe. Digital Satellite Television (DSTV) is also available by subscribing to *MultiChoice.*

Toilets / Restrooms

Toilets are labeled in English, and sometimes in Shona:

Women   *Vakadzi*
Men   *Varume*

Electricity

Electricity is generated at 220/240V. Appliances from the United States will require a transformer.

Food and Drink

The local staple food is *sadza*, a thick porridge made using maize meal. It is usually served with either beef, chicken, pork, or fish and vegetables. Normally people use their hands while eating sadza. The washing of hands before touching food is an important aspect of Shona culture.

There are many restaurants that offer international cuisine, especially in Harare. There are also a number of familiar fast-food outlets, such as KFC.

Zimbabwe produces beer and wine locally. A wide variety of wines are also imported from Australia, South Africa and Europe.

Health

Medical services in Zimbabwe are generally quite good and medical equipment is sterilized. The major cities have excellent hospitals and one would have no problems in seeking adequate medical attention. There are also private and public clinics that normally require cash payments for patients who do not hold medical insurance cards. Pharmacies can be found easily in major towns. However, a doctor's prescription is required because there is a strict policy towards selling medicine.

When traveling to malaria-prone zones, it is advisable to take malaria pills and to use mosquito repellent to reduce one's chances of getting malaria.

THE
SHONA
LANGUAGE

The Shona language belongs to the Bantu language group. The Bantu languages form part of the great Niger-Congo language family that extends from the west of Africa in the Senegal Valley to the Kenyan coast and south to Namibia and the eastern Cape in Southern Africa. The Bantu branch is the predominant language group in most of Africa south of the equator and is made up of languages that have been recognized since the sixteenth century as being remarkably similar in grammatical structure and vocabulary. Linguists have concluded that Bantu languages spread from a common region within the last three or four thousand years.

Shona (also referred to as ChiShona) is the native language of 80 percent of Zimbabwe's population (pop. circa twelve million). The language is fairly uniform throughout the country and local dialects are mutually intelligible. The Shona dialects, namely Zezuru, Karanga, Manyika, Korekore and Ndau, provide ethnic identity.

The Shona language in written form has a relatively short history. The term "Shona" is a linguistic creation that dates back to 1930.

The first whites to visit Zimbabwe were missionaries, adventurers and concession seekers. It was the missionaries who played a crucial role in putting the oral forms into written form. The different missionary societies in Zimbabwe during this time (late nineteenth and early twentieth centuries) strove to translate the Bible into the local languages. Towards that aim, each missionary group attempted to study the languages that were spoken around their mission stations. Together they formed the Southern Rhodesia Missionary Conference to discuss issues pertaining to reducing the local languages into writing. After two decades of meetings, they still failed to agree on a standard written form for the local languages.

In 1929, the missionaries agreed to recommend to the government the hiring of a trained linguist to come and study the language situation, as well as to make recommendations on how to transcribe these languages. Professor Clement Doke, a phonetician from South Africa, was commissioned to do the work. In 1930 Professor Doke published a *Report on the Unification of the Shona Dialects*. From 1930 on, the term "Shona" has been used to cover what could potentially have been classified into separate languages. Doke recommended that "Shona" should be separated into five dialects: Zezuru, Karanga, Manyika, Ndau and Korekore, all of which are mutually intelligible.

The majority of the population is bilingual in Shona or Ndebele, and English. Ndebele, along with Shona, belongs to the Bantu language family that originated in the Niger/Congo region, and is spoken by about 20 percent of the population, mostly in Matebeleland in the western and southwest parts of the country. The government also officially recognizes five minority languages: Kalanga, Tonga, Nambya, Venda and Shangana. These languages are spoken mainly in the border areas of the country.

English is the official language used in education, administration, justice, trade and commerce. Shona is used as a medium of instruction up to the third grade. Thereafter, it is taught as a subject up to the tertiary level.

Shona is also spoken in neighboring Mozambique, Zambia and South Africa.

ABBREVIATIONS

sg.	singular
pl.	plural
v.	verb
LT	Low Tone
HT	High Tone

ALPHABET AND PRONUNCIATION

The Shona Alphabet[1]

Shona Letter	Shona Name of Letter
A	a
B	ba
Bh	bha
Ch	cha
D	da
Dh	dha
E	e
F	fa
G	ga
H	ha
I	i
J	ja
K	ka
M	ma
N	na
Nh	nha
O	o
P	pa
R	ra
S	sa
Sh	sha
T	ta

---

1. Mawadza, A. *Shona Dictionary and Phrasebook.* (New York: Hippocrene Books, 2000), 9.

U	u
V	va
Vh	vha
W	wa
Y	ya
Z	za
Zh	zh

Pronunciation Guide[2]

Shona Letter	Shona Example	Gloss	Approximate English Equivalent
a	amai	Mother, Mrs.	account
b	baba	father	—
bh	bhazi	bus	butter
ch	chenji	change	change
d	dada	be proud	—
dh	dhadha	duck	doll
e	enda	to go	edit
f	famba	walk *v.*	food
g	gara	to sit, stay, live	gum
h	hongu	yes	horse
i	inwa	drink *v.*	ink
j	jamu	jam	jug
k	kora	collar	collar
m	mira	stop *v.*	meat
n	nama	seal *v.*	neat
nh	nhau	news	—
o	ona	to see	orange
p	pasi	floor, ground	pack
r	rara	sleep *v.*	—
s	sarudza	to choose	sit
sh	shanda	work *v.*	shoe
t	taura	to speak	tone
u	uya	come	ululate
v	vakadzi	women	—
vh	vhara	close *v.*	valentine
w	iwe	you	we
y	yadhi	yard	yard
z	zai	egg	zip
zh	zhizha	summer	pleasure

2. Mawadza, p. 10.

Vowels

There are five vowels in Shona. Pronunciation is relatively easy, as it does not vary.

Shona Vowel	Shona Example	Gloss	Approximate English Equivalent
a	amai	mother	abroad
e	enda	go	egg
i	imba	house	important
o	ona	see	orange
u	uya	come	rule

Syllables

Some Shona syllables are difficult to pronounce. These are syllables that represent those sounds that are not found in English. For example, **sw** is pronounced "skw."

Other examples

bv	**kubva**	to come from
bw	**Zimbabwe**	Zimbabwe
dy	**kudya**	to eat
mv	**mvura**	water
mw	**mwana**	child
nw	**kunwa**	to drink
ny	**nyora**	to write
sv	**svika**	to arrive
ty	**tyora**	to break
zv	**zvino**	now
zw	**izwi**	word, voice

Semi-vowels

There are three semi-vowels in the Shona language: **w, y, v.**

The semi-vowels **w** and **y** are pronounced very lightly, as in:

uya	come
yamwa	breast-feed
wana	get; marry
vana	children

Tone

The Shona language has two basic tones, "high" and "low" (high pitch vs. low pitch), and these provide a contrast in meaning. For example, *guru* means either "huge" (high tone) or "third stomach of ruminant" (low tone). Not every syllable is pronounced in a high or low tone.[3]

---

3. Mawadza, p. 13.

EXERCISES

I.   Read the following words.

kubva, kudya, mvura, mwana, nyora, zvino, izwi, Zimbabwe, svika, tyora

II. Read the following words, paying attention to the vowels.

enda, amai, uya, ona, imba

III. Read the following words.

baba, vhara, nhau, inwa, hongu, gara, zai, iwe, rara, mira, taura, famba, bhazi

LESSON
ONE

DIALOGUE

Kusuma

Mwanasikana ari kusuma shamwari yake kuna amai.

TENDAI: Masikati amai.

AMAI: Masikati Tendai. Waswera sei?

TENDAI: Ndaswera kana maswerawo amai.

AMAI: Ndaswera.

CHIPO: Mhoroi.

AMAI: Mhoro mwanangu. Wakadini?

CHIPO: Tiripo kana makadiniwo.

AMAI: Tiripo.

TENDAI: Amai, uyu anonzi Chipo. Ishamwari yangu uye anodzidza kuUniversity.

AMAI: Ndafara kukuziva Chipo.

CHIPO: Neniwo ndafara.

AMAI: Unobva kupi?

CHIPO: Ndinobva kuChivhu.

AMAI: Zvakanaka. Vabereki vako vanogara kupi?

CHIPO: Vabereki vangu vanogara kuChivhu.

AMAI: KuUniversity unodzidza chii?

CHIPO: Ndiri kuita dhigirii reChiShona.

AMAI: Zvakanaka.

Introductions

A daughter is introducing a friend to her mother.

TENDAI: Good afternoon mother.

AMAI: Good afternoon, Tendai. How did you spend the day?

TENDAI: I spent the day well, how about you?

AMAI: I spent the day well.

CHIPO: Hello.

AMAI: Hello, my child. How are you?

CHIPO: I am fine, how about you?

AMAI: I am fine.

TENDAI: Mother, this is Chipo. She is my friend and she studies at the University.

AMAI: I am happy to know you, Chipo.

CHIPO: Me, too.

AMAI: Where do you come from?

CHIPO: I come from Chivhu.

AMAI: All right. Where do your parents live?

CHIPO: My parents live in Chivhu.

AMAI: What do you study at the University?

CHIPO: I am doing a degree in Shona.

AMAI: All right.

VOCABULARY

amai	mother
ari	she is
chii?	what?
Chipo	personal name
dhigirii	degree
ishamwari	he / she / it is my friend
kana	if
kubva	to come from
kuChivhu	from Chivhu (place name)
kudzidza	to learn / study
kufara	to be happy
kugara	to live / stay / sit
kuita	to do
kuna	to (a person)
kunzi	to be called
kupi?	where?
kusuma	to introduce
kuswera	to spend the day
kuUniversity	at the University
kuziva	to know
masikati	afternoon
mwanangu	my child
mwanasikana	daughter
ndiri	I am
neniwo	and me too
reChiShona	of ChiShona
sei?	how?
shamwari	friend
Tendai	personal name
uye	and
uyu	this

vabereki	parents
vako	your
vangu	my
yake	his/her
yangu	my

EXPRESSIONS

Masikati.	Good afternoon.
Mhoroi.	Hello. (formal / plural form)
Mhoro.	Hello. (informal / singular form)
Makadini?	How are you? (formal / plural)
Wakadini?	How are you? (informal / singular)
Tiripo kana makadiniwo.	We are fine, how about you?
Tiripo.	We are fine.
Ndafara kukuziva.	I am happy to know you.
Neniwo.	And me too.
Zvakanaka.	All right.

GRAMMAR

Personal Pronouns

The following are the personal pronouns. It is not necessary to use these pronouns with the verb except for emphasis. The subject prefix (see below) suffices, as it also indicates the pronoun. When emphasis is needed, the pronoun and subject prefix are used together.

There is no distinction of gender in Shona. Thus *iye* can refer to a man or a woman. However, it cannot be used to refer to "it" as the neuter third person does not exist in Shona.

Notice the two different Shona translations of "you." *Iwe* is the familiar or friendly "you" that is used when talking with children, friends or younger people. *Imi* is the plural and polite / formal "you" used for addressing more than one person or older people, superiors or people we do not know very well.

Person	Singular		Plural	
1st	**Ini**	I	**Isu**	We
2nd	**Iwe**	You	**Imi**	You (polite)
3rd	**Iye**	He / She	**Ivo**	They

Subject Prefixes

The basic subject prefixes given below are used with the present and future tenses. (The corresponding personal pronoun is noted in italics.)

Person	Singular		Plural	
1st	*Ini*	Ndi-	*Isu*	Ti-
2nd	*Iwe*	U-	*Imi*	Mu-
3rd	*Iye*	A-	*Ivo*	Va-

Emphatic Pronouns

Emphatic pronouns are formed by reduplicating (repeating) the second syllable of the personal pronoun. The purpose of reduplication is for emphasizing the reference being made to a certain subject, for example, "I personally...," "You personally...".

Inini	I personally
Isusu	We personally
Iwewe	You (*sg.*) personally
Imimi	You (*pl.*) personally
Iyeye	He/She personally
Ivavo	They personally

Addressing People

When meeting a person for the first time, one uses the polite form of address *imi*. There is no written starting age for this but normally by the age of six one will start using the polite form when addressing people. The polite / formal form is used unless both parties decide and agree on the familiar form. First names are used mostly among friends, otherwise the last name and the polite form is used.

Multiple-Word Units

Words are formed by combining multiple words to make a single unit. For instance, *ndinodya* (I eat) is made up of the following:

ndi-   I (1st person singular)
-no-   present tense marker
-dya   eat (verb stem)

Word Order

The structure of Shona is relatively simple. Word order is flexible and the verb is usually at the beginning of the sentence after the subject.

Ndinodya chingwa mazuva ose.
I eat bread every day.

Infinitive Verbs

The infinitive of the verb is marked by **ku-**, for example, *kudya* = to eat.

Present Tense and Negation
basic subject prefix + *no* + verb stem

Present tense conjugation of *dya* (eat):

e.g. **Ndi + no + dy + a**

Ndinodya   I eat
Unodya   You eat
Anodya   He / She eats

Tinodya	We eat
Munodya	You eat
Vanodya	They eat

Formation of the negative present tense

The formation of the negative differs from one verb tense to another. In the present tense, **ha-** is the negative marker and the **-a** verb stem ending changes to **-i**. The **-i** verb stem ending occurs with the negative of some tenses, but not all.

The negative is formed as follows:

Ha + basic subject prefix + verb stem (ending in *i*)

e.g. **Ha + ndi + dy + i**

Handidyi	I do not eat
Haudyi	You do not eat
Haadyi	He / She does not eat
Hatidyi	We do not eat
Hamudyi	You do not eat
Havadyi	They do not eat

Present Progressive Tense and Negation

The present progressive tense in Shona is equivalent to the English "verb + -ing." This tense is formed as follows:

basic subject prefix + *ri* + infinitive verb

e.g. **Ndi + ri + kudya**

Ndiri kudya	I am eating
Uri kudya	You are eating
Ari kudya	He / She is eating
Tiri kudya	We are eating
Muri kudya	You are eating
Vari kudya	They are eating

Formation of the negative present progressive tense

The negative is formed as follows:

Ha + basic subject prefix + *si* + infinitive verb

e.g. **Ha + Ndi + si + kudya**

Handisi kudya	I am not eating
Hausi kudya	You are not eating
Haasi kudya	He / She is not eating
Hatisi kudya	We are not eating
Hamusi kudya	You are not eating
Havasi kudya	They are not eating

EXERCISES

I.   Give the negative forms for the following sentences.

1. Ndiri kudya.
2. Tendai anodzidza ChiShona.
3. Vanoenda.
4. Uri kudya.
5. Tinodzidza History.

II. Translate.

1. How are you?
2. Where do you live?
3. What do you study?
4. Good afternoon.
5. Hello.
6. My friend.
7. Pleased to know you.
8. My name is Tendai.
9. All right.
10. How did you spend the day?

III. Convert the following negative sentences into the affirmative form.

1. Handidzidzi Shona.
2. Havadyi chingwa.
3. Hamubvi kuAmerica.
4. Hatiendi kuZimbabwe.
5. Haaendi kuUniversity.

IV. Give the basic subject prefixes for the following pronouns.

1. Ini
2. Isu
3. Iwe
4. Imi
5. Iye
6. Ivo

V. Practice and translate the following conversation.

1. Masikati.
2. Maswera sei?
3. Taswera maswerawo.
4. Vabereki vako vanogara kupi?
5. Unodzidza chii kuUniversity?
6. Ndafara kukuziva.

LESSON TWO

DIALOGUE

Kubvunza nzira

TENDAI: Pamusoroi, ndingabvunzawo here?

CHIPO: Hongu, bvunzai zvenyu.

TENDAI: Ndarasika, ndiri kutsvaga mabhazi anoenda kuZengeza. Ndingaawane kupi?

CHIPO: Mabhazi anoenda kuZengeza anowanikwa paCharge Office.

TENDAI: Charge Office iri kupi?

CHIPO: Iri muna Robson Manyika Avenue.

TENDAI: Ndinosvika sei ikoko?

CHIPO: Endai nemugwagwa uyu, endai kurudyi pamunosvika paunogumira.

TENDAI: Ndatenda chaizvo.

CHIPO: Muchitendei.

Asking for Directions

TENDAI: Excuse me, may I ask?

CHIPO: Yes, you may ask.

TENDAI: I am lost. I am looking for buses that go to Zengeza. Where can I get them?

CHIPO: Buses that go to Zengeza are found at the Charge Office.

TENDAI: Where is the Charge Office?

CHIPO: It is along Robson Manyika Avenue.

TENDAI: How do I get there?

CHIPO: Go along this road; turn right when you get to the end of that road.

TENDAI: Thank you very much.

CHIPO: You are welcome.

VOCABULARY

bvunzai	ask (-*i* "you" plural or honorific)
chaizvo	very much
endai	you go
here	(interrogative marker)
hongu	yes
ikoko	there
iri	it is
kubvunza	to ask
kuenda	to go
kupi	where
kurasika	to get lost
kurudyi	to the right
kutenda	to thank
kutsvaga	to look for
kuwana	to find
kuwanikwa	to be found
kuZengeza	to Zengeza (place name)
mabhazi	buses
muna	along
ndinosvika	I get
ndiri	I am
nemugwagwa	along the road
paCharge Office	at the Charge Office
pamunosvika	when you get
pamusoroi	excuse me
paunogumira	to the end
Robson Manyika Avenue	(street name)
sei?	how?
uyu	this
zvenyu	referring to "you" (*pl.*)

EXPRESSIONS

Pamusoroi.	Excuse me.
Ndingabvunzewo here?	May I ask?
Hongu.	Yes.
Bvunzai zvenyu.	You may ask.
Ndatenda chaizvo.	(I) thank you very much.
Muchitendei.	You are welcome.

GRAMMAR

Imperative Verbs

The imperative of the verb occurs in two forms, singular and plural. The singular form of the imperative is used when giving commands to children or in informal situations. The plural form is used when addressing adults, strangers, or more than one person. Monosyllabic verbs like -*dya* (eat) and -*nwa* (drink) are prefixed with the vowel /i/ when they function as imperatives.

	Imperative		
Verb Stem	Singular	Plural	
bvunza (ask)	bvunza	bvunzai	(Ask.)
famba (walk)	famba	fambai	(Walk.)
taura (speak)	taura	taurai	(Speak.)
mira (stop)	mira	mirai	(Stop.)
-dya (eat)	idya	idyai	(Eat.)
-nwa (drink)	inwa	inwai	(Drink.)

Negative Commands: Expressing "Do not . . ."

Negative commands are formed as follows:

basic subject prefix + *sa* + verb stem (ending -*e*)

U + sa + fambe = *Usafambe!* (Do not walk!) (*sg.*)
Mu + sa + fambe = *Musafambe!* (Do not walk!) (*pl.*)

U + sa + dye = *Usadye!* (Do not eat!) (*sg.*)
Mu + sa + dye = *Musadye!* (Do not eat!) (*pl.*)

The Verbs "to be" and "to have" and Negation

- *kuri* "to be"

The verb "to be" takes the **-ri** form with the first and second persons. (It cannot be used in the third person.) This verb is used to express gender, race, status, profession, nationality and religion. Hence it is used for self-identification.

construction: basic subject prefix + *-ri*

Singular	Plural
Ndiri (I am)	Tiri (We are)
Uri (You are)	Muri (You are)

EXAMPLES:

Ndiri mukadzi.	I am a woman.
Ndiri muchena.	I am a white person.
Ndiri mudzidzisi.	I am a teacher.
Ndiri muAmerican.	I am an American.
Ndiri muCatholic.	I am Catholic.

The negative form of "to be" is constructed as follows:

Ha + basic subject prefix + *-si*

Singular	Plural
Handisi (I am not)	Hatisi (We are not)
Hausi (You are not)	Hamusi (You are not)

EXAMPLES:

Handisi mukadzi.	I am not a woman.
Hatisi vadzidzi.	We are not students.
Hamusi mupfupi.	You are not short.

- *kune* "to have"

In Shona the verb "to have" is an irregular verb signifying "to be with."

construction: basic subject prefix + *-ne*

Singular	Plural
Ndine (I have)	Tine (We have)
Une (You have)	Mune (You have)
Ane (He / She has)	Vane (They have)

EXAMPLES:

Ndine nzara.	I am hungry. (lit. "I am with / have hunger.")
Tine nyota.	We are thirsty.

"To have" can also be used to express ailments and diseases:

Ndine musoro.	I have a headache.
Ane zino.	He / She has a toothache.

Note that the affirmative *-ne* shifts to *-na* in the negative. The negative form is constructed as follows:

Ha + basic subject prefix + *-na*

Singular	Plural
Handina (I do not have)	Hatina (We do not have)
Hauna (You do not have)	Hamuna (You do not have)
Haana (He / She does not have)	Havana (They do not have)

EXAMPLES:

Handina nzara.	I am not hungry.
Hatina nyota.	We are not thirsty.

The Verb "to have" and Weather Terms

Kune "to have" is used to describe the weather. Thus:

Noun	With Verb "to have"	Gloss
zuva	kune zuva	there is sunshine
chando	kune chando	... cold
makore	kune makore	... clouds
mvura	kune mvura	... rain
mheni	kune mheni	... lightning
mhepo	kune mhepo	... wind

EXERCISES

I. Complete the following sentences.

  1. Ndi _____ muAmerican.
  2. Ti _____ vadzidzi.
  3. Mabhazi anowanikwa _____ ?
  4. Ku _____ mhepo here?
  5. Ndino _____ Shona.

II. Translate.

  1. May I ask?
  2. Yes.
  3. You may ask.
  4. Thank you very much.
  5. All right.
  6. You are welcome.

III. Give the negative forms of the following words.

  1. famba
  2. taura
  3. dzidza
  4. tenga
  5. fara
  6. sevenza
  7. enda

IV. Complete the following table.

Verb	Imperative Singular	Imperative Plural	Meaning
bvunza	_____	_____	Ask.
taura	_____	_____	Speak.
-dya	_____	_____	Eat.
famba	_____	_____	Walk.
mira	_____	_____	Stop.

V. Practice the following conversation.

1. Pamusoroi, munotaura Shona here?
2. Hongu, ndinotaura Shona.
3. Mabhazi anoenda kuZengeza anowanikwa kupi?
4. PaCharge Office.
5. Ndatenda.
6. Zvakanaka.

LESSON
THREE

DIALOGUE

Kuembassy

TENDAI: Masikati.

OFFICER: Maswera sei?

TENDAI: Ndaswera kana maswerawo.

OFFICER: Ndaswera. Ndingakubatsire nei?

TENDAI: Ndiri kuda visa yekuenda kuAmerica. Ndiri kuenda kuchikoro. Mapepa angu aya.

OFFICER: Zvakanaka. Visa iUS$100. Inotora zuva rimwe chete.

TENDAI: Oyi mari.

OFFICER: Ndipe pasipoti yako. Udzoke mangwana.

TENDAI: Nguvai?

OFFICER: Na12 masikati.

TENDAI: Mazvita.

At the Embassy

TENDAI: Good afternoon.

OFFICER: How did you spend the day?

TENDAI: I spent it well, if you spent it well too.

OFFICER: I spent it well. How can I help you?

TENDAI: I want a visa to go to America. I am going to school. These are my papers.

OFFICER: All right. A visa costs US$100. It will be ready in one day.

TENDAI: Here is the money.

OFFICER: Give me the passport. You come back tomorrow.

TENDAI: At what time?

OFFICER: At twelve in the afternoon.

TENDAI: Thank you.

VOCABULARY

chete	only
iUS$100	it is US$100
kana	if
kubatsira	to help
kuda	to want
kudzoka	to come back
kuonana	to see each other
kupa	to give
kuswera	to spend the day
kutora	to take
mangwana	tomorrow
mari	money
masikati	good afternoon
mazvita	thank you
ndiri	I am
nei	with what
oyi	here is (interjective of giving)
pasipoti	passport
rimwe	one
sei?	how?
visa	visa
yako	your
zuva	day

EXPRESSIONS

Masikati.	Good afternoon.
Maswera sei?	How did you spend the day?
Ndingakubatsire nei?	How can I help you?
Nguvai?	At what time?
Mazvita.	Thank you.

GRAMMAR

Past Tense

There are three forms of the past tense in Shona: the recent past, the remote past and the progressive past. The following past subject prefixes are used with all of the past tenses.

Past subject prefixes

Person	Singular		Plural	
1st	*Ini*	**Nda-**	*Isu*	**Ta-**
2nd	*Iwe*	**Wa-**	*Imi*	**Ma-**
3rd	*Iye*	**A-**	*Ivo*	**Va-**

Recent past tense and negation

The recent past tense is used to refer to an action that has just ended or that happened on the day in question.

construction: past subject prefix + verb stem

Nda + enda = *Ndaenda* (I went)
Wa + enda = *Waenda* (You went)

Formation of the negative recent past tense

The negative of the recent past tense is formed as follows:

Ha + basic subject prefix + *na* (negative particle) + infinitive verb

Ha + ndi + na + kuenda = *Handina kuenda* (I did not go)
Ha + u + na + kuenda = *Hauna kuenda* (You did not go)

Remote past tense and negation

The remote past tense refers to an action that occurred the day before or further in the past. This tense is used to describe a definite past occurrence.

construction: past subject prefix + *ka* + verb stem

Nda + ka + enda = *Ndakaenda* (I went)
Wa + ka + enda = *Wakaenda* (You went)

Formation of the negative remote past tense

The negative form of the remote past tense is the same as that of the recent past:

Ha + basic subject prefix + *na* + infinitive verb

Handina kuenda (I did not go)

Progressive past tense and negation

The progressive past tense refers to an action that was performed habitually in the past.

construction: past subject prefix + *i* + verb stem

Nda + i + enda = *Ndaienda* (I used to go)
Wa + i + enda = *Waienda* (You used to go)

Formation of the negative progressive past tense

construction: *Ha* + past subject prefix + *i* + verb stem

Ha + nda + i + enda = *Handaienda* (I did not use to go)
Ha + wa + i + enda = *Hawaienda* (You did not use to go)

Future Tense and Negation

The future tense is used to refer to an action that will be performed
in the future. The basic subject prefixes used for the present tense
are also used to form the future tense.

construction: basic subject prefix + *cha* + verb stem

Ndi + cha + enda = *Ndichaenda* (I will go)
U   + cha + enda = *Uchaenda* (You will go)

Formation of the negative future tense

construction: *Ha* + basic subject prefix + *cha* + verb stem (ending in *i*)

Ha + ndi + cha + endi = *Handichaendi* (I will not go)
Ha + u   + cha + endi = *Hauchaendi* (You will not go)

The negative form of the future also expresses the meaning of "no
longer . . .".

The Stative Tense

The stative **-ka-** indicates a complete state of being, for instance a state of being full, clever, beautiful, etc. It is always formed with the past subject prefix, but indicates a present state or condition.

construction: past subject prefix + *ka* + verb stem

<u>EXAMPLES</u>:

Ndakangwara	I am clever
Wakanaka	You are beautiful
Akaguta	He / She is full

The negative of this tense is formed in exactly the same way as the negative of the recent and remote past tenses.

EXERCISES

I.   Negate the following.

  1. Ndafamba.
  2. Vaenda.
  3. Taidzidza.
  4. Wakanwa.
  5. Adya.

II. Translate the following sentences.

  1. Good afternoon.
  2. Can I help you?
  3. How did you spend the day?
  4. We will see each other.
  5. Give me the money.

III. Give the future tense forms for the following verbs.

  1. Ndakaenda.
  2. Aenda.
  3. Vakadzidza.
  4. Wanwa.
  5. Mataura.

IV. Give the past subject prefixes for the following pronouns.

  1. Ini
  2. Isu
  3. Iwe
  4. Imi
  5. Iye
  6. Ivo

V. Practice and translate the following conversation.

1. Masikati.
2. Masikati.
3. Maswera sei?
4. Ndaswera kana maswerawo.
5. Ndaswera.
6. Ndingakubatsire nei?
7. Ndinoda kutora pasipoti.
8. Zvakanaka.

LESSON
FOUR

DIALOGUE

Hotera

CHIPO: Manheru.

ATTENDANT: Manheru, maswera sei?

CHIPO: Taswera kana maswerawo.

ATTENDANT: Ndingakubatsirei nei?

CHIPO: Ndiri kuda imba yekurara.

ATTENDANT: Muri vangani?

CHIPO: Ini nemwana wangu.

ATTENDANT: Mwana wenyu ane makore mangani?

CHIPO: Maviri.

ATTENDANT: Munoda kugara mazuva mangani?

CHIPO: Matatu.

ATTENDANT: Zvakanaka, iZW$1520. Muchagara murumu 301.

CHIPO: Mazvita.

Hotel

CHIPO: Good evening.

ATTENDANT: Good evening, how did you spend the day?

CHIPO: I spent it well, if you spent it well too.

ATTENDANT: How can I help you?

CHIPO: I want a room for the night.

ATTENDANT: How many are you?

CHIPO: Me and my child.

ATTENDANT: How old is your child?

CHIPO: Two.

ATTENDANT: How many days do you want to stay?

CHIPO: Three.

ATTENDANT: All right. It is ZW$1520. You will stay in room 301.

CHIPO: Thank you.

VOCABULARY

ane	he / she has
iZW$1520	it is ZW$1520
imba	house
Ini	me; I
kana	if
kubatsira	to help
kuda	to want
kugara	to stay
kurara	to sleep
kuswera	to spend the day
makore	years
mangani	how many
manheru	good evening
matatu	three
maviri	two
mazuva	days
mazvita	thank you
muri	you are
murumu	in room
mwana	child
ndiri	I am
nei	with what
nemwana	and child
vangani	how many
wangu	my
wenyu	your
zvakanaka	all right

EXPRESSIONS

Manheru.	Good evening.
Maswera sei?	How did you spend the day?
Ndingakubatsire nei?	How can I help you?
Mazvita.	Thank you.
Zvakanaka.	All right.

GRAMMAR

Numbers

Shona numerals follow the decimal system. The Shona people count from ONE to TEN as follows:

poshi	one
piri	two
tatu	three
ina	four
shanu	five
tanhatu	six
nomwe	seven
sere	eight
pfumbabwe	nine
gumi	ten

Time

Inguvai?	What time is it?
I-three o'clock.	It is three o'clock.
I-ten o'clock.	It is ten o'clock.
I-hafu past three.	It is half past three.

Days of the Week

Muvhuro	Monday
Chipiri	Tuesday
Chitatu	Wednesday
China	Thursday

Chishanu	Friday
Mugovera	Saturday
Svondo	Sunday

The Shona language uses the preposition **ne-** to mean "on":

neMuvhuro	on Monday
neMugovera	on Saturday

Months of the Year

Ndira	January
Kukadzi	February
Kurume	March
Kubvumbi	April
Chivabvu	May
Chikumi	June
Chikunguru	July
Nyamavhuvhu	August
Gunyana	September
Gumiguru	October
Mbudzi	November
Zvita	December

Asking and Giving the Date

Nhasi chingani?	What day is it today?
Nhasi Chipiri.	Today is Tuesday.
Mangwana chingani?	What day is it tomorrow?
Mangwana Chitatu.	Tomorrow is Wednesday.
Nhasi dheti chii?	What is the date today?
Nhasi ndi5 Kukadzi.	Today is the 5th of February.

| *Zuva* | day |
| *Nezuro* | yesterday |

Svondo	week
Svondo rino	this week
Svondo rinouya	next week
Svondo rakapera	last week

Mwedzi	month
Mwedzi uno	this month
Mwedzi unouya	next month
Mwedzi wakapera	last month

Gore	year
Gore rino	this year
Gore rinouya	next year
Gore rakapera	last year

Cardinal Directions

Chamhembe	North
Maodzanyemba	South
Mabvazuva	East
Madokero	West

Seasons

Mwaka	season
Zhizha	rainy season (November–March)
Chirimo	warm dry season (September–October)
Chando	cold weather (April–August)

EXERCISES

I. Review the imperative singular and plural forms of the following verbs.

1. kuda
2. kurara
3. kuswera
4. kugara
5. kubatsira
6. kubvunza

II. Translate the sentences.

1. What day is it today?
2. Tomorrow is Tuesday.
3. How old are you?
4. Today is Wednesday.
5. What is the date today?

III. Practice and translate the following conversation.

1. Manheru.
2. Manheru.
3. Ndiri kuda imba yekurara.
4. Zvakanaka, muri vangani?
5. Tiri vaviri. Inoita marii?
6. IZW$1520.
7. Mazvita.

LESSON FIVE

DIALOGUE

Pamusika

TENDAI: Masikati.

MUKADZI: Masikati, mwanangu, ndingakubatsire nei?

TENDAI: Ndinoda kutenga, mune chii?

MUKADZI: Ndine mabhanana, maorenji, muriwo nemaapuro.

TENDAI: Ndipeiwo mabhanana matatu, nemuriwo, imarii?

MUKADZI: IZW$200 chete.

TENDAI: I-ii, zviri kudhura!

MUKADZI: Zvinhu zviri kudhura mazuva ano mwanangu.

TENDAI: Oyi mari yenyu.

MUKADZI: Ndatenda, chenji yako iZW$20.

TENDAI: Zvakanaka, chisarai ndava kuenda.

MUKADZI: Tatenda.

At the Market

TENDAI: Good afternoon.

WOMAN: Good afternoon my child, how can I help you?

TENDAI: I want to buy, what do you have?

WOMAN: I have bananas, oranges, vegetables and apples.

TENDAI: Give me three bananas and some vegetables. How much is it?

WOMAN: It's only ZW$200.

TENDAI: I-ii, they are expensive!

WOMAN: Things are expensive nowadays, my child.

TENDAI: Here is your money.

WOMAN: Thank you, your change is ZW$20.

TENDAI: All right, good-bye, I am going.

WOMAN: Thank you.

VOCABULARY

ano	these
chenji	change
chete	only
chii	what
chisarai	good-bye
iZW$200	it is ZW$200
iZW$20	it is ZW$20
I-ii	(exclamation of surprise)
imarii	how much is it?
kubatsira	to help
kuda	to want
kudhura	to be expensive
kuenda	to go
kutenda	to thank
kutenga	to buy
mabhanana	bananas
maorenji	oranges
mari	money
masikati	good afternoon
matatu	three
mazuva	days
mune	you have
muriwo	vegetables
mwanangu	my child
ndava	I am about
ndipeiwo	give me
-ne	have
nei	with what
nemaapuro	and apples
nemuriwo	and vegetables
oyi	here is (interjective of giving)

yako	your (*sg.*)
yenyu	your (*pl.*)
zvakanaka	all right
zvinhu	things
zviri	they are

EXPRESSIONS

Maswera sei?	How did you spend the day?
Imarii?	How much is it?
Ndipeiwo.	Give me.
Zvakanaka	All right, OK
Chisarai.	Good-bye.
Tatenda.	Thank you.

GRAMMAR

Noun Categories and the Shona Noun Class System

Nouns in Shona are divided into different categories, e.g. people, trees, animals, things, abstract, etc. The nouns are grouped according to their meaning and number (singular/plural). The noun's prefix signifies the class to which the noun belongs. As such, each noun class has a noun prefix. For example, singular nouns belonging to the "people" category begin with **mu-**.

The order of presentation below is based on the noun class system.

Also given in the charts below are the basic subject prefixes (for present and future tenses) and the past subject prefixes (for past tenses) that correspond to each category. These subject prefixes accompany verbs and agree in category and number with the noun to which they refer. For example, "people" category nouns as the subject of a verb require that the verb in question take either the singular prefix **a-** or the plural prefix **va-**.

In the following example, *munhu* (person) is a "people" category singular noun and therefore takes the **mu-** "people" category singular prefix. *Anotaura* (speaks) is the verb prefixed by **a-**, the appropriate "people" category subject prefix, which represents the noun.

Munhu anotaura.   A person speaks.

"People" category nouns

Nouns in this category refer to people. Singular nouns take the prefix
mu- and plural nouns take the prefix va-. The singular prefix mu-
changes to mw- before noun stems that begin with a vowel.

Noun	Basic Subject Prefix (present & future tenses)	Past Subject Prefix (past tenses)
(*sg.*)	a-	a-
mukomana "boy"		
munhu "person"		
musikana "girl"		
mwana "child"		
(*pl.*)	va-	va-
vakomana "boys"		
vanhu "people"		
vasikana "girls"		
vana "children"		

EXAMPLES:

Munhu anotaura.	A person speaks.
Vanhu vanotaura.	People speak.
Munhu akataura.	A person spoke.
Vanhu vakataura.	The people spoke.

"Tree" category nouns

Nouns in this category refer to trees, plants, or parts of the body.

As with the "people" category nouns, **mu-** changes to **mw-** before noun stems that begin with a vowel ("vowel-initial stems").

Noun	Basic Subject Prefix	Past Subject Prefix
(sg.)	**u-**	**wa-**
muti "tree"		
muuyu "baobab tree"		
mwedzi "month," "moon"		
(pl.)	**i-**	**ya-**
miti "trees"		
miuyu "baobab trees"		
mwedzi "months," "moons"		

EXAMPLES:

Muti unokura.	A tree grows.
Miti inokura.	Trees grow.
Muti wakakura.	A tree grew.
Miti yakakura.	The trees grew.

Hard-sounding nouns

Nouns in this category refer to fruits, body parts, and animals, as well as borrowings from other languages, especially English. "Hard-sounding" refers to the sound on the ear when the word is pronounced. The nouns in this category do not have an overt prefix. The prefix only surfaces in agreement; i.e., the basic / past subject prefix on the verb stem.

Noun	Basic Subject Prefix	Past Subject Prefix
(*sg.*)	ri-	ra-
banga "knife"		
bhazi "bus"		
bveni "baboon"		
dare "court"		
dhongi "donkey"		
dzimba "animal footprint"		
gudo "baboon"		
jira "cloth"		
rize "scorpion"		
sango "forest"		
zai "egg"		
(*pl.*)	a-	a-
mazai "eggs"		

In the plural forms, "ma" is added and the following consonant changes occur:

b	→	p
bv	→	pf
dz	→	ts
d	→	t
g	→	k
j	→	ch

Therefore:

banga (knife)	mapanga (knives)
dare (court)	matare (courts)
jira (cloth)	machira (cloths)
gudo (baboon)	makudo (baboons)
bveni (baboon)	mapfeni (baboons)
dzimba (animal footprint)	matsimba (animal footprints)

EXAMPLES:

Banga riri kupi?	Where is the knife?
Banga raenda kupi?	Where did the knife go?
Mapanga ari kupi?	Where are the knives?
Mapanga aenda kupi?	Where did the knives go?

"Things" category nouns

Nouns in this category represent objects, especially of small size, and tools, as well as verbal derivations, such as *chigero* (scissors). The verb here is -*gera* (shave).

The singular and plural prefixes for nouns in this category are **chi-** (singular) and **zvi-** (plural).

Noun	Basic Subject Prefix	Past Subject Prefix
(sg.)	**chi-**	**cha-**
chikoro "school"		
chikwama "wallet"		
chingwa "bread"		
chinhu "thing"		
chipo "gift"		
chitoro "store"		
(pl.)	**zvi-**	**zva-**
zvikoro "schools"		
zvikwama "wallets"		
zvingwa "breads"		
zvinhu "things"		
zvipo "gifts"		
zvitoro "stores"		

EXAMPLES:

Chingwa chiri kupi?	Where is the bread?
Chingwa chaenda kupi?	Where did the bread go?
Mary atora chigero changu.	Mary took my scissors.

Light-sounding nouns

This category includes animals, miscellaneous "light-sounding" nouns, as well as borrowings. Like the hard-sounding nouns, the nouns in this category do not have an overt prefix. The prefix surfaces in sentence agreement (and indicates whether the noun is singular or plural).

Noun	Basic Subject Prefix	Past Subject Prefix
(*sg.*)	**i-**	**ya-**
tsamba "letter"		
hama "relative"		
imbwa "dog"		
nzou "elephant"		
katsi "cat"		
pikicha "picture"		
mombe "cow"		
shumba "lion"		
nyika "country"		
(*pl.*)	**dzi-**	**dza-**
tsamba "letters"		
hama "relatives"		
imbwa "dogs"		
nzou "elephants"		
katsi "cats"		
pikicha "pictures"		
mombe "cows"		
shumba "lions"		
nyika "countries"		

EXAMPLES:

Tsamba ichaenda rinhi?	When will the letter go?
Tsamba dzichaenda rinhi?	When will the letters go?
Tsamba yakaenda rinhi?	When did the letter go?
Tsamba dzakaenda rinhi?	When did the letters go?

Nouns referring to long things

Nouns in this category refer to long or thin objects, e.g. *ruoko* (hand). When verbs are modified to become nouns with abstract meanings, they also fall into this category, e.g. *ruvengo* (hatred) derived from the verb -*venga* (hate).

The singular noun prefix is **ru-** and it changes to **rw-** before a noun beginning with a vowel. The plural prefix is **ma-**, which is only used for non-abstract nouns (abstract nouns do not have a plural form).

Noun	Basic Subject Prefix	Past Subject Prefix
(*sg.*)	**ru- / rw-**	**rwa-**
ruoko "hand" rufaro "happiness" rugare "peace" ruvengo "hatred"		
(*pl.*)	**ma-**	**ma-**
Only for non-abstract nouns: maoko "hands"		

EXAMPLES:

Ruoko <u>ru</u>ri kurwadza.	The hand is painful (hurts).
Maoko <u>a</u>ri kurwadza.	The hands are painful (hurt).

Diminutive nouns

Nouns of this category refer to diminutive beings and objects.

The noun prefixes are **ka-** for the singular and **tu-** for the plural. In this category, **tu-** changes to **tw-** before vowel-initial stems.

Noun	Basic Subject Prefix	Past Subject Prefix
(*sg.*)	**ka-**	**ka-**
kakomana "little boy"		
kamwana "little child"		
kasikana "little girl"		
(*pl.*)	**tu- / twu-**	**twa-**
tukomana "little boys"		
tusikana "little girls"		
tuvana "little children"		

EXAMPLES:

Kasikana <u>ka</u>ri kutamba.	The little girl is dancing.
Tusikana <u>twa</u>katamba.	The little girls danced.

Abstract nouns

This category refers to abstract nouns, for example *upfumi* (wealth).

The singular noun prefix **u-** changes to **hw-** with vowel-initial stems. These nouns only occur in the singular form because they refer to abstract, non-countable things.

Noun	Basic Subject Prefix	Past Subject Prefix
(*sg.*)	**u- / hwu-**	**hwa-**
upenyu "life"		
urombo "poverty"		
uroyi "witchcraft"		
(*pl.*)	–	–

EXAMPLES:

Upfumi <u>hwu</u>ri kupi?	Where is the wealth?
Upfumi <u>hwa</u>kaenda kupi?	Where did the wealth go?

Verbal nouns

Nouns of this class have the **ku-** verbal prefix and refer to a "way of doing," for example, *kufamba* (walking). Nouns in this class do not have a plural form.

Noun	Basic Subject Prefix	Past Subject Prefix
(*sg.*)	**ku-**	**kwa-**
kubvunza "asking"		
kufamba "walking"		
kuseka "laughing"		
kutamba "dancing," "playing"		
(*pl.*)	–	–

EXAMPLE:

Kubvunza kwakanaka.	Asking is a good thing.

Locative nouns

The nouns in this category refer to all types of locations.

These nouns are prefixed with **pa-**, **ku-**, or **mu-**, meaning "at / on,"
"to / from / towards," and "in / inside," respectively. Thus:

pachikoro	at school
kuchikoro	to school
muchikoro	in school

Noun	Basic Subject Prefix	Past Subject Prefix
Locative prefixes		
pa- "at"	**pa-**	**pa-**
ku- "to / from / towards"	**ku-**	**kwa-**
mu- "in"	**mu-**	**ma-**

EXAMPLES:
Pachikoro pedu apo.   There is our school.
Ndiri kubva kuchikoro.   I am coming from school.

Diminutives (Karanga)

This category is used only in the Karanga dialect of Shona, and refers
to diminutives, for example *svisikana* (little girls).

Noun	Basic Subject Prefix	Past Subject Prefix
(*sg.*)	**svi-**	**sva-**
svimbwa "little dog"		
svirume "little boy"		
(*pl.*)	**a-**	**sva-**
svisikana "little girls"		

Examples:

Svirume <u>svi</u>ri kupi?	Where is the small boy?
Svisikana <u>sva</u>enda rinhi?	When did the little girls go?

Argumentative / pejorative nouns

Nouns in this category refer to big (and huge) things. In this case, the prefixes **zi-** (singular) and **ma-** (plural) indicate the size and / or stature of the noun.

Noun	Basic Subject Prefix	Past Subject Prefix
(*sg.*)	**ri-**	**ra-**
zisikana "big girl"		
zimbwa "big dog"		
zirume "big man"		
(*pl.*)	**a-**	**a-**
mazimbwa "big dogs"		
mazirume "big men"		
mazisikana "big girls"		

Examples:

Zirume <u>ra</u>enda.	The huge man has gone.
Mazirume <u>a</u>enda.	The huge men have gone.

EXERCISES

I.   Give the plural forms of the following nouns.

    1. musikana
    2. mwana
    3. banga
    4. zai
    5. munhu
    6. tsamba
    7. kakomana
    8. upenyu
    9. chikwama
  10. urombo

II.   Complete the sentences using the correct subject prefix.

    1. Banga _____ri kupi?
    2. Mapanga _____ri kupi?
    3. Tsamba _____ri kupi? (*sg.*)
    4. Tsamba _____ri kupi? (*pl.*)
    5. Kasikana _____ri kupi?
    6. Tusikana _____ri kupi?

III. Translate the following words and phrases.

    1. good-bye
    2. to be expensive
    3. give me
    4. How much is it?
    5. We are about to go.

IV. Practice and translate the following conversation.

1. Pamusoroi.
2. Ndingakubatsirei nei?
3. Ndinoda kutenga mabhanana nemuriwo.
4. IZW$500.
5. Ndipeiwo muriwo.
6. Zvakanaka.

LESSON
SIX

DIALOGUE

Kufamba

TENDAI: Masikati.

MUTYAIRI: Masikati, muri kuenda kupi?

TENDAI: Ndinoda kuenda kutaundi.

MUTYAIRI: Pindai tiende.

TENDAI: Imarii kusvikako?

MUTYAIRI: IZW$100 chete.

TENDAI: Ho-o, kwava kudhura chaizvo.

MUTYAIRI: Ndiyoyo mari yacho mazuva ano.

TENDAI: Nhai? Ndiburutsei pano.

MUTYAIRI: Papi?

TENDAI: Padyo nebhangi.

MUTYAIRI: Okeyi.

TENDAI: Oyi mari yenyu. Ndatenda chaizvo.

MUTYAIRI: Muchitendei.

Traveling

TENDAI: Good afternoon.

DRIVER: Good afternoon, where are you going?

TENDAI: I want to go to town.

DRIVER: Enter, let us go.

TENDAI: How much is it to get there?

DRIVER: It's only ZW$100.

TENDAI: O-o, it is now very expensive.

DRIVER: That is the money nowadays.

TENDAI: Is it? Drop me off here.

DRIVER: Where?

TENDAI: Near the bank.

DRIVER: All right.

TENDAI: Here is your money. Thank you.

DRIVER: You're welcome.

VOCABULARY

ano	these
burutsa	drop
chaizvo	very / very much
chete	only
Ho-o	(interjection)
iZW$100	it is ZW$100
imarii?	how much is it?
kuda	to want
kudhura	to be expensive
kuenda	to go
kufamba	to travel
kupi	where
kupinda	to enter
kusvikako	to get there
kutaundi	to town
kutenda	to thank
kwava	it is now
mari	money
masikati	good afternoon
mazuva	days
mutyairi	driver
ndiyoyo	it is
nebhangi	the bank
nhai?	is it?
okeyi	okay
oyi	here is (interjective of giving)
padyo	near
pano	here
papi	(at) where
yacho	(referring to "the money")
yenyu	your

EXPRESSIONS

Ndiburutsei.	Drop me off.
Muchitendei.	You are welcome.
Okeyi.	OK.

GRAMMAR

The Article

Shona does not have definite or indefinite articles. Translation into English depends on context.

Ndakatenga bhuku.   I bought a book.
Ndakaverenga mabhuku.   I read the books.

The Possessive

Possession of nouns is expressed in Shona by combining the appropriate possessive stem (which indicates person) with a possessive prefix. The prefix used is determined by the category of the possessed noun. The possessive stands on its own as a word, and follows the noun to which it refers.

mwana wangu   my child
vana vangu   my children

The possessive stems:

Singular		Plural	
-ngu	my	**-edu**	our
-ko	your	**-enyu**	your
-ke	his / her	**-vo**	their

Possessives with "people" category nouns

The possessive prefix occurs as a single consonant, such as **v-**, when the possessive stem begins with a vowel; e.g., *v-enyu* (your).

Noun	Possessive Prefix	Possessive Stem
(*sg.*)		
mukomana "boy"	**wa-**	**-ngu**
munhu "person"	**wa-**	**-ko**
musikana "girl"	**wa-**	**-ke**
mwana "child"	**w-**	**-edu**
	w-	**-enyu**
	wa-	**-vo**
(*pl.*)		
vakomana "boys"	**va-**	**-ngu**
vanhu "people"	**va-**	**-ke**
vasikana "girls"	**v-**	**-edu**
vana "children"	**va-**	**-ko**
	v-	**-enyu**
	va-	**-vo**

EXAMPLES:

mwana wake	his / her child
vana vake	his / her children
vanhu vangu	my people

With "tree" category nouns

Noun	Possessive Prefix	Possessive Stem
(sg.)		
muti "tree"	wa-	-ngu
mwedzi "month", "moon"	wa-	-ko
	wa-	-ke
	w-	-edu
	w-	-enyu
	wa-	-vo
(pl.)		
miti "trees"	ya-	-ngu
mwedzi "months", "moons"	ya-	-ko
	ya-	-ke
	y-	-edu
	y-	-enyu
	ya-	-vo

EXAMPLES:
muti wangu   my tree
miti yedu   our trees

With hard-sounding nouns

Noun	Possessive Prefix	Possessive Stem
(*sg.*)		
banga "knife"	ra-	-ngu
bhazi "bus"	ra-	-ko
dare "court"	ra-	-ke
dhongi "donkey"	r-	-edu
gudo "baboon"	r-	-enyu
jira "cloth"	ra-	-vo
rize "scorpion"		
sango "forest"		
zai "egg"		
(*pl.*)		
mazai "eggs"	a-	-ngu
	a-	-ko
	a-	-ke
	(no prefix)	-edu
	(no prefix)	-enyu
	a-	-vo

EXAMPLES:

jira rangu	my cloth
banga ravo	their knife
mazai ake	his / her eggs

With "things" category nouns

Noun	Possessive Prefix	Possessive Stem
(sg.)		
chikoro "school"	cha-	-ngu
chikwama "wallet"	cha-	-ko
chingwa "bread"	cha-	-ke
chinhu "thing"	ch-	-edu
chipo "gift"	ch-	-enyu
chitoro "store"	cha-	-vo
(pl.)		
zvikoro "schools"	zva-	-ngu
zvikwama "wallets"	zva-	-ko
zvingwa "breads"	zva-	-ke
zvinhu "things"	zv-	-edu
zvipo "gifts"	zv-	-enyu
zvitoro "stores"	zva-	-vo

With light-sounding nouns

Noun	Possessive Prefix	Possessive Stem
(*sg.*)		
hama "relative"	ya-	-ngu
imbwa "dog"	ya-	-ko
katsi "cat"	ya-	-ke
mombe "cow"	y-	-edu
nzou "elephant"	y-	-enyu
pikicha "picture"	ya-	-vo
shumba "lion"		
tsamba "letter"		
(*pl.*)		
hama "relatives"	dza-	-ngu
	dza-	-ko
	dza-	-ke
	dz-	-edu
	dz-	-enyu
	dza-	-vo

Examples:

tsamba yako	your letter
tsamba dzako	your letters
hama yenyu	your relative
hama dzenyu	your relatives

As shown by the above examples, singular and plural nouns in this category are distinguished by the possessive prefix. Hence "ya-" in *tsamba yako* signifies the singular, while "dza-" in *tsamba dzako* signifies the plural.

With nouns referring to long things

Noun	Possessive Prefix	Possessive Stem
(*sg.*)		
ruoko "hand"	rwa-	-ngu
	rwa-	-ko
	rwa-	-ke
	rw-	-edu
	rw-	-enyu
	rwa-	-vo
(*pl.*)		
maoko "hands"	a-	-ngu
	a-	-ko
	a-	-ke
	(no prefix)	-edu
	(no prefix)	-enyu
	a-	-vo

Note: The plural is only used for non-abstract nouns.

With diminutive nouns

Noun	Possessive Prefix	Possessive Stem
(sg.)		
kakomana "little boy"	ka-	-ngu
kamwana "little child"	ka-	-ko
kasikana "little girl"	ka-	-ke
	k-	-edu
	k-	-enyu
	ka-	-vo
(pl.)		
tukomana "little boys"	twa-	-ngu
twana "little children"	twa-	-ke
tusikana "little girls"	twa-	-ko
	tw-	-edu
	tw-	-enyu
	twa-	-vo

<u>EXAMPLES</u>:
kasikana kangu   my little girl
tusikana twangu   my little girls

With abstract nouns

Noun	Possessive Prefix	Possessive Stem
(*sg.*)		
upenyu "life"	hwa-	-ngu
upfumi "wealth"	hwa-	-ko
urombo "poverty"	hwa-	-ke
	hw-	-edu
	hw-	-enyu
	hwa-	-vo
(*pl.*)	—	—

EXAMPLES:
upfumi hwake   his / her wealth
upenyu hwangu   my life

With verbal nouns

Noun	Possessive Prefix	Possessive Stem
(*sg.*)		
kudya "eating"	kwa-	-ngu
kufamba "traveling"	kwa-	-ko
kuseka "laughing"	kwa-	-ke
kutamba "playing," "dancing"	kw-	-edu
	kw-	-enyu
	kwa-	-vo
(*pl.*)	—	—

EXAMPLES:
kufamba kwake   his / her way of walking
kutamba kwavo   their way of dancing

With locative nouns

(a) *ku-* locative "to," "from," "towards"

Noun	Possessive Prefix	Possessive Stem
(sg.)		
kuchikoro "to / from /	kwa-	-ngu
towards the school"	kwa-	-ko
kumba "to / from /	kwa-	-ke
towards the house"	kw-	-edu
	kw-	-enyu
	kwa-	-vo
(pl.)	—	—

EXAMPLES:

Tiri kuenda kuchikoro kwedu.	We are going to our school.
Uya kumba kwangu.	Come to my house.

(b) *pa-* locative "at," "on"

Noun	Possessive Prefix	Possessive Stem
(sg.)		
pachikoro "at the school"	pa-	-ngu
pamba "at the house"	pa-	-ko
	pa-	-ke
	p-	-edu
	p-	-enyu
	pa-	-vo
(pl.)		
	pa-	-ngu
	pa-	-ko
	pa-	-ke
	p-	-edu
	p-	-enyu
	pa-	-vo

(c) *mu-* locative "in," "inside"

Noun	Possessive Prefix	Possessive Stem
(*sg.*)		
muchikoro "in / inside	ma-	-ngu
the school"	ma-	-ko
mumba "in the house"	ma-	-ke
	m-	-edu
	m-	-enyu
	ma-	-vo

EXAMPLES:

Pinda mumba mangu.	Get inside my house.
Tarisa muchikoro medu.	Look inside our school.

With diminutives (Karanga)

Noun	Possessive Prefix	Possessive Stem
(*sg.*)		
svana "little child"	sva-	-ngu
svisikana "little girl"	sva-	-ko
	sva-	-ke
	sv-	-edu
	sv-	-enyu
	sva-	-vo
(*pl.*)	—	—

EXAMPLES:

svana svangu	my little child
svisikana svenyu	your little girl

With argumentative / pejorative nouns

Noun	Possessive Prefix	Possessive Stem
(sg.)		
zirume "big man"	ra-	-ngu
zisikana "big girl"	ra-	-ko
	ra-	-ke
	r-	-edu
	r-	-enyu
	ra-	-vo
(pl.)		
mazirume "big men"	a-	-ngu
mazisikana "big girls"	a-	-ko
	a-	-ke
	(no prefix)	-edu
	(no prefix)	-enyu
	a-	-vo

EXAMPLES:

zisikana rangu	my big girl
zirume rako	your big man

EXERCISES

I. Complete the phrases with the correct possessive prefix.

   1. Mazai _____ngu.
   2. Mwana _____enyu.
   3. Kamwana _____ke.
   4. Upenyu _____vo.
   5. Zvinhu _____edu.
   6. Bhuku _____ko. ("bhuku" is hard category)
   7. Mumba _____vo.
   8. Upenyu _____ke.
   9. Pikicha _____ngu. (sg.)
   10. Zvipo _____ko.

II. Translate the terms and phrases.

   1. my child
   2. Enter into my house.
   3. his little girl
   4. We are going to our school.
   5. We are coming from their school.

III. Practice and translate the following conversation.

   1. Masikati, munoda kuenda kupi?
   2. Ndinoda kuenda kuUniversity.
   3. Zvakanaka.
   4. Imarii kusvika kuUniversity?
   5. IZW$200 chete.
   6. Oyi ZW$200.
   7. Ndatenda, fambai zvakanaka.

LESSON
SEVEN

DIALOGUE

Kutambira Vaeni

Vaeni: Gogoi, Tisvikewo!

Tendai: Svikai. Pindai. Garai pasi.

Vaeni: Mhoroi.

Tendai: Mhoroi. Makadini?

Vaeni: Tiripo makadiniwo.

Tendai: Tiripo. Vakadii vamwe kwamabva?

Vaeni: Varipo zvavo.

Tendai: Regai ndikubikirei sadza.

Vaeni: A-a musanetseke, takaguta.

Tendai: A-a chokwadi here? Ko tii?

Vaeni: Zvakanaka.

Tendai: Inwai tii.

Vaeni: Tatenda.

Welcoming Visitors

VISITORS: Knock, knock! May we come in?

TENDAI: You may come in. Enter. Sit down.

VISITORS: Hello.

TENDAI: Hello. How are you?

VISITORS: We are fine and you?

TENDAI: We are fine. How are the others where you are from?

VISITORS: They are fine.

TENDAI: Let me cook some sadza for you.

VISITORS: A-a, do not bother, we are full.

TENDAI: A-a, really? What about tea?

VISITORS: All right.

TENDAI: Have some tea.

VISITORS: Thank you.

VOCABULARY

chokwadi	truth
garai	sit
gogoi	knock, knock
here	(interrogative marker)
inwai	(you) drink
ko	what about
kuguta	to be full
kusvika	to arrive
kutambira	to receive
kutenda	to thank
kwamabva	where you came from
makadini	how are you?
makadiniwo	how are you? (also)
mhoroi	hello
musanetseke	(you) do not bother
ndikubikirei	cook for you
pasi	down
pindai	enter
regai	let me
sadza	sadza (staple food in Zimbabwe)
svikai	you may come in
tii	tea
tiripo	we are fine
vaeni	visitors
vakadii	how are they
vamwe	others
varipo	they are fine
zvakanaka	all right
zvavo	(referring to "them")

EXPRESSIONS

Gogoi.	Knock, knock.
Mhoroi.	Hello.
Makadini.	How are you?
Tiripo.	We are fine.
Pindai.	You may enter.
Tatenda.	Thank you.
Takaguta.	We are full.

GRAMMAR

Demonstratives

Demonstratives are used to point out or specify a person or thing. The following "space demonstratives" are used to describe a person or thing near the speaker. The demonstrative agrees with the category and number of the noun to which it refers, as given in the chart below.

The demonstrative is placed after the noun.

Noun Category	this / these	that / those
People		
sg. munhu "person"	uyu	uyo
pl. vanhu "people"	ava	avo
Trees		
sg. muti "tree"	uyu	uyo
pl. miti "trees"	iyi	iyo
Hard-Sounding		
sg. banga "knife"	iri	iro
pl. mapanga "knives"	aya	ayo
Things		
sg. chinhu "thing"	ichi	izvi
pl. zvinhu "things"	izvi	izvo
Light-Sounding		
sg. hama "relative"	iyi	iyo
pl. (same)	idzi	idzo

Long things
sg. ruoko "hand"   urwu   urwo
pl. maoko "hands"   aya   ayo

Diminutive
sg. kasikana "little girl"   aka   ako
pl. tusikana "little girls"   utwu   utwo

Abstract
upenyu "life"   uhwu   uhwo

Verbal
sg. kudya "way of eating food"   uku   uko

Locative
pa- "at"   apa   apo
ku- "to," "from," "towards"   uku   uko
mu- "in," "inside"   umu   umo

Diminutive (*Karanga*)
svikomana "little boy"   isvi   isvo

Argumentative
sg. zirume "huge man"   iri   iro
pl. mazirume "huge men"   aya   ayo

EXAMPLES:
musikana uyu   this girl
miti iyi   these trees
kasikana aka   this little girl
zirume iro   that huge man

Descriptives—Adjectives

Shona, like other Bantu languages, has only a few words that can be described as "pure adjectives." These adjectives denote color, size / dimension, quantity / number, and quality / state.

Color

-tsvuku	red, maroon	*-tema*	black, dark
-chena	white	*-pfumbu*	grey
-shava	brown	*-shora*	yellow

Size

-kuru	big, large, adult, fully grown	*-diki*	small, little, young
-zhinji	many, much	*-shoma*	few, little
-refu	tall, long	*-pfupi*	short
-pamhi	broad	*-tete*	thin
-kobvu	fat, thick	*-hombe*	big

EXAMPLES:

Ndatenga kapu tsvuku.	I bought a red cup.
Ane mari zhinji.	He has a lot of money.
mwana mudiki	a small child
musikana murefu	a tall girl

In the last two examples given, the adjective is accompanied by the prefix **mu-**, in agreement with the respective nouns. The first two examples do not have this requirement because their nouns do not carry an overt prefix.

Quality

Stative adjectives typically denote qualities and physical properties.

-naka	be sweet/beautiful
-vava	be bitter
-ibva	be ripe
-ngwara	be wise/clever

Quantity (numerical)

-mwe	one	*-viri*	two
-tatu	three	*-na*	four
-shanu	five	*-tanhatu*	six
-nomwe	seven	*-sere*	eight
-pfumbamwe	nine	*-gumi*	ten

Descriptives—Quantitatives

Quantitative adjectives qualify nouns and pronouns. In normal word order, quantitatives come after the nouns that they modify. Quantitatives can be reduplicated for emphasis.

There are three quantitative stems in Shona:

-se the whole of, all   **-ga** alone   **-mene** self

EXAMPLES:

vanhu vose	all people
nyika yose	the whole country
ndega	I alone
tega	we alone
iye womene	he himself
ivo vomene	they themselves

EXERCISES

I. Complete the following sentences using the right form of the
    demonstrative.

    1. Mwana _____ achaenda. (this)
    2. Bhazi _____ rava kuenda. (that)
    3. Musikana _____ auya rinhi? (that)
    4. Ndinoda hembe _____ . (this)
    5. Vakomana _____ vanogara naani? (these)

II. Translate.

    1. The whole country.
    2. A very tall person.
    3. Those people.
    4. I alone.
    5. Many people.

III. Translate the phrases.

    1. I came alone.
    2. He himself went.
    3. All the people ate.
    4. a very few days
    5. a short girl

IV. Practice the following conversation.

1. Gogoi, Tisvikewo!
2. Svikai. Pindai. Garai pasi.
3. Mhoroi.
4. Mhoroi. Makadini?
5. Tiripo makadiniwo.
6. Tiripo.
7. Vakadii vamwe?
8. Varipo.

LESSON
EIGHT

DIALOGUE

Kukoka

TENDAI: Hallo Chipo!

CHIPO: Hesi Tendai, uri bho-o here?

TENDAI: Shamwari, ini ndiri raiti.

CHIPO: Saka ndeipi?

TENDAI: Shamwari, ndiri kuda kukukoka kupati kumba kwedu.

CHIPO: Ipati yei?

TENDAI: Ye*Christmas*, ichaitwa musi weChishanu manheru.

CHIPO: Waita zvako shamwari, ndichasvika musi weChishanu.

TENDAI: Zvakanaka.

CHIPO: Horaiti shamwari.

Invitation

TENDAI: Hello, Chipo!

CHIPO: Hi Tendai, how are you?

TENDAI: My friend, I am fine.

CHIPO: So, what's up?

TENDAI: My friend, I want to invite you to a party at our house.

CHIPO: A party to celebrate what?

TENDAI: For Christmas; it will be held on Friday evening.

CHIPO: Thank you, friend, I will be there on Friday.

TENDAI: All right.

CHIPO: All right, friend.

VOCABULARY

bho-o	good (slang, informal)
hallo	hello
here?	(interrogative marker requiring a yes / no response)
hesi	hi
horaiti	all right
ini	I
ipati	it is a party
kuda	to want
kufona	to phone / call
kuita	did
kuitwa	to be held (passive)
kukoka	to invite
kukukoka	to invite you
kumba	to the house
kupati	to a party
kusvika	to arrive
kutenda	to thank
kwedu	our
manheru	evening
musi	day
ndeipi?	what's up?
ndiri	I am
raiti	all right
saka	so
shamwari	friend
uri	you are
weChishanu	on Friday
ye*Christmas*	for Christmas
yei	for what
zvakanaka	all right
zvako	(referring to "you")

EXPRESSIONS

Ndeipi?	What's up?
Ndiri raiti.	I am fine.
Horaiti.	All right.
Ndatenda.	Thank you.

GRAMMAR

Special Constructions

Special constructions include terms for expressing "still . . ." "can I?" and "about to . . .". These constructions are useful for everyday conversation.

- **Still ...**

    basic subject prefix + *chiri* + infinitive form of the verb

    EXAMPLES:
Ndichiri kudya.	I am still eating.
Vachiri kuenda here?	Are they still going?
Tichiri pano.	We are still here.

- **Can I ...**

    basic subject prefix + *nga* + verb (ending in *-e*) + *wo*

    EXAMPLES:
Ndingabvunzewo here?	Can I ask?
Ndingataurewo nemi here?	Can I speak with you?
Tingauyewo here?	Can we come?
Angataurewo here?	Can he / she speak?

    Note that *here* is a question tag requiring a "yes" / "no" response.

- **About to ...**

    past subject prefix + *va* + infinitive form of the verb

EXAMPLES:

Ndava kudya.	I am about to eat.
Tava kuenda.	We are about to go.
Bhazi rava kuenda.	The bus is about to go.
Mabhazi ava kuenda.	The buses are about to go.

Expressing "about to ..." using different noun categories

Noun Category	Expressing "about to ..."
People	
sg. munhu "person"	ava
pl. vanhu "people"	vava
Trees	
sg. muti "tree"	wava
pl. miti "trees"	yava
Hard-Sounding Nouns	
sg. banga "knife"	rava
pl. mapanga "knives"	ava
Things	
sg. chinhu "thing"	chava
pl. zvinhu "things"	zvava
Light-Sounding	
sg. mombe "cow"	yava
pl. mombe "cows"	dzava
Long Things	
sg. ruoko "hand"	rwava
pl. maoko "hands"	ava

Diminutive
sg. kasikana "little girl"   **kava**
pl. twusikana "little girls"   **twava**

Abstract
sg. upenyu "life"   **hwava**

Verbal
sg. kudya "way of eating, food"   **kwava**

Locative
pamba "at the house"   **pava**
kumba "to / from / toward the house"   **kwava**
mumba "in the house"   **mava**

Diminutive (*Karanga*)
svikomana "little boy"   **svava**

Argumentative
sg. zirume "big man"   **rava**
pl. mazirume "big men"   **ava**

EXAMPLES:

Mombe yava kudya.	The cow is about to eat.
Mombe dzava kudya.	The cows are about to eat.
Kasikana kava kuuya.	The little girl is about to come.
Tusikana twava kuuya.	The little girls are about to come.

EXERCISES

I. Give the Shona equivalents for the following.

    1. All right.
    2. What's up?
    3. I am fine.
    4. He is still eating.
    5. Can I come?

II. Use the first person plural marker to construct sentences using the verb "to eat" with the following expressions.

    1. "Can we ..."
    2. "Still ..."

III. Make requests using the following verbs with the first person singular.

    e.g. *Ndingaendewo here?* Can I go?

    1. bvunza
    2. gara
    3. taura
    4. batsira
    5. enda

IV. Practice the following conversation.

    1. Hesi Tendai, ndeipi?
    2. Hapana.
    3. Ndinoda kukukoka kupati.
    4. Zvakanaka shamwari, rinhi?

5. Musi weChina.
6. Pati iri nguvai?
7. Inotanga na6.30 manheru.
8. Zvakanaka ndinouya.
9. Ndatenda.

LESSON
NINE

DIALOGUE

Kutenga

VASIKANA: Pamusoroi, tingabvunzewo here?

MUTENGESI: Bvunzai zvenyu.

VASIKANA: Tiri kuda kutenga bhuku rinonzi rengano.

MUTENGESI: Rakanyorwa naani?

VASIKANA: Hatizivi.

MUTENGESI: Regai nditsvage.

MUTENGESI: Hatina.

VASIKANA: Tingariwane kupi?

MUTENGESI: Edzai TextBook Sales.

VASIKANA: Iri kupi?

MUTENGESI: TextBook Sales iri muna Angwa Street.

VASIKANA: Tatenda chaizvo.

MUTENGESI: Zvakanaka.

Shopping

Girls:	Excuse me, may we ask?
Bookseller:	You may ask.
Girls:	We want to buy a book of folktales.
Bookseller:	Who wrote it?
Girls:	We do not know.
Bookseller:	Let us look for it.
Bookseller:	We do not have it.
Girls:	Where can we get it?
Bookseller:	Try TextBook Sales.
Girls:	Where is it?
Bookseller:	TextBook Sales is along Angwa Street.
Girls:	Thank you very much.
Bookseller:	All right.

VOCABULARY

Angwa Street	(street name)
bhuku	book
bvunzai	you may ask
chaizvo	very much
hatina	we do not have
here?	(interrogative)
iri	it is
kubvunza	to ask
kuda	to want
kunyorwa	to be written
kupi?	where?
kutenda	to thank
kutenga	to buy
kutsvaga	to look for
kuwana	to get
kuziva	to know
muna	along
mutengesi	seller
naani?	by whom?
ngano	folktale
pamusoroi	excuse me
regai	let me
rinonzi	that is called
TextBook Sales	(place name)
tiri	we are
vasikana	girls
zvakanaka	all right
zvenyu	(referring to "you")

EXPRESSIONS

Pamusoroi.	Excuse me.
Bvunzai.	You may ask.
Tatenda chaizvo.	Thank you very much.

GRAMMAR

Question Words

Question words are a way of asking for information. There are various devices in Shona for marking questions. The first involves tone or syllable length changes. As such, there may not be any perceivable difference in writing between a statement and an *information question*. A second device used to indicate a question or to ask for information is with the use of question words.

The clearest way of indicating a question in Shona is by the use of the *here* question marker which is put at the end of the sentence. The *here* question marker in Shona requires a yes/no answer.

Unotaura Shona here?	Do you speak Shona?
Mwana adya here?	Has the child eaten?
Muri kuuya here?	Are you coming?
Tichaenda kuchikoro here?	Are we going to school?

The Interrogative chii: *what*

The word *chii* can occur at the beginning or end of a sentence. It asks the question "what?"

Anoda chii?	What does he/she want?
Chii ichi muShona.	What is this in Shona?
Muri kubika chii?	What are you cooking?
Wati chii?	What did you say?

The Interrogative i: *what, what kind of, how much*

The interrogative *i* occurs as a suffix marker on the main word in a question. It asks the questions "what?" "what kind of?" or "how much?"

Inguvai?	<u>What</u> time is it?
Imarii?	<u>How much</u> is it?

The Interrogative ani: *who*

Ani: "who" refers to "people" category nouns and has the plural form *vanaani* when asking about a series of names. (It is the only interrogative word with a plural form.) It can be attached to the subject as a suffix, or it can be a separate word.

Ndiani?	<u>Who</u> is it?
Ndivanaani?	<u>Who</u> are they?
Ndiwe ani?	<u>Who</u> are you?
Wauya naani	With <u>whom</u> did you come?

Note that it is *ani* (and not *chii* "what") that is used when asking about a person's name or the names of entities (rivers, bridges, etc.)

Unonzi ani?	<u>What</u> is your name?
Mwana uyu anonzi ani?	<u>What</u> is the name of this child?
Mhuri yenyu inonzi ani?	<u>What</u> is your family name?
Rwizi urwu runonzi ani?	<u>What</u> is the name of this river?

The Time Interrogative rinhi: *when*

The interrogative *rinhi* asks the question "when?" It is placed at the end of a sentence and never occurs at the beginning.

Auya <u>rinhi</u>?	<u>When</u> did she/he come?
Muchaenda <u>rinhi</u>?	<u>When</u> will you go?
Tichasvika <u>rinhi</u>?	<u>When</u> are we arriving?
Wakazvarwa <u>rinhi</u>?	<u>When</u> were you born?

However, the word **nguvai** is used ask the time (as mentioned above).

The Place Interrogative pi: *where*

Questions about place or location are formed with the locative interrogative suffix -*pi* "where?" *Pi* occurs with the locative prefixes *ku-* (to, from, towards), *mu-* (in), and *pa-* (at, on).

Anobva <u>kupi</u>?	<u>Where</u> does s/he come from?
Zviri kurwadza <u>papi</u>?	<u>Where</u> does it hurt?
Munogara <u>kupi</u>?	<u>Where</u> do you live?
Tichagara <u>mupi</u>?	<u>Where</u> (inside) will we live?

However, with prefixes other than the locatives, the interrogative -*pi* signifies "which one?" Thus:

Mwana u<u>pi</u>?	<u>Which</u> child?
Banga ri<u>pi</u>?	<u>Which</u> knife?

The Quantity Interrogative ngani: *how many*

Ngani indicates a question of quantity: "how many?"

Une makore ma<u>ngani</u>?	<u>How</u> old are you?
Unoda mabhuku ma<u>ngani</u>?	<u>How many</u> books do you want?
Munoda vadzidzi va<u>ngani</u>?	<u>How many</u> students do you want?

The Reason Interrogative sei: *why, how*

Sei asks the question "why" when it occurs at the beginning of the sentence.

<u>**Sei**</u> **wauya?**	<u>Why</u> did you come?
<u>**Sei**</u> **ari kuchema?**	<u>Why</u> is he/she crying?

When it occurs at the end of the sentence, *sei* means "how?" Thus:

Wauya <u>sei</u>?	<u>How</u> did you come?
Warara <u>sei</u>?	<u>How</u> did you sleep?
Waswera <u>sei</u>?	<u>How</u> did you spend the day?

EXERCISES

I. Translate.

1. How much is it?
2. What time is it?
3. How did you go?
4. How old are you?
5. When did you come?

II. Complete the following phrases using the correct interrogative form.

1. Unotaura Shona _____ ?
2. Unonzi _____ ?
3. Tichaenda kuchikoro _____ ?
4. Makarara _____ ?
5. Vanogara _____ ?

III. Practice and translate the following conversation.

1. Pamusoroi, tinoda kutenga bhuku.
2. Bhuku rinonzi chii?
3. Rinonzi History of Zimbabwe.
4. Ndine urombo, hatina.
5. Zvakanaka, tatenda chaizvo.

LESSON
TEN

DIALOGUE

Kudya Kwemanheru

TENDAI:	Manheru baba.
BABA:	Manheru Tendai, waswera sei?

TENDAI:	Ndaswera kana maswerawo.
BABA:	Ndaswera, kuchikoro kwakadii?
TENDAI:	Kuri raiti. *Maths* ndidzo dziri kunetsa.
BABA:	Wotoshingirira mwanangu.
TENDAI:	Ndichaedza.

Patafura

AMAI:	Uyai mudye.
BABA:	Zvakanaka.
AMAI:	Gezai maoko.
BABA:	Pamusoroi.
AMAI:	Idyai. Torai nyama.
BABA:	Chikafu chiri kunaka. Ndiani abika?
AMAI:	NdiTendai. Tendai wava kugona kubika mwanangu.

TENDAI:	Ndatenda baba.
BABA:	Ndipeiwo mvura yekunwa.
AMAI NABABA:	Wazvita Tendai, taguta chaizvo.
TENDAI:	Muchitendei.

Dinner

TENDAI:	Good evening, father.
FATHER:	Good evening Tendai, how did you spend the day?
TENDAI:	I spent it well, if you spent it well too.
FATHER:	I spent it well; how is school?
TENDAI:	It was fine. Math is the problem.
FATHER:	You have to persevere, my child.
TENDAI:	I will try.

At the table

MOTHER:	Come and eat.
FATHER:	All right.
MOTHER:	Wash your hands.
FATHER:	Excuse me.
MOTHER:	Eat. Take some, eat.
FATHER:	The food is good. Who cooked?
MOTHER:	It is Tendai. Tendai, you are now able to cook, my child.
TENDAI:	Thank you, father.
FATHER:	Give me some water to drink.
MOTHER and **FATHER:**	Thank you Tendai, we are so full.
TENDAI:	You are welcome.

VOCABULARY

amai	mother
baba	father
chaizvo	very much
chikafu	food
chiri	it is
dziri	that is
gezai	wash (*pl., hon.*)
idyai	eat (*pl., hon.*)
kana	if
kubika	to cook
kuchikoro	school
kudya	eat, to eat (verbal noun)
kuedza	to try
kugona	to be able
kuguta	to be full
kunaka	to taste good
kunetsa	to be a problem
kupa	to give
kuri	it is
kushingirira	to persevere
kuswera	to spend the day
kutenda	to thank
kwakadii?	how was it?
kwemanheru	of evening
manheru	evening
maoko	hands
Maths	Math
muchitendei	you are welcome
mvura	water
mwanangu	my child
ndiani	who

ndidzo	is the one
ndiTendai	it is Tendai
nyama	meat
pamusoroi	excuse me
patafura	at the table
raiti	right
sei?	how?
torai	take (*pl., hon.*)
uyai	come (*pl.*)
wava	you are now
wazvita	thank you
yekunwa	to drink
zvakanaka	all right

EXPRESSIONS

Manheru.	Good evening.
Gezai maoko.	Wash your hands.
Ndipeiwo.	Give me (*polite*).
Muchitendei.	You are welcome.
Taguta.	We are full.
Uya tidye.	Come and eat
Taswera kana maswerawo.	I spent it well if you spent it well too.

GRAMMAR

Conjunctions

The conjunction is used to link words, phrases, clauses, or sentences.

Conjunction	Meaning
asi	but
kana	if, or, when, even
kubvira	ever since
kudakara/*kudzimara*	until
kuti	so that
na-/*ne-*	and, with
naizvozvo	hence, so
nekuti	because
saka	so
uye	and
zvimwe	maybe, otherwise
zvino	then

N.B.: The conjunction *na-*/*ne-* is used when combining two nouns.
The conjunction *na-* is used when joining proper nouns and *ne-* is
used when joining common nouns. The conjunction *uye* is used
when combining two ideas.

Ndinoda kuimba asi handidi kutamba.	I like singing but I do not like to dance.
Unoda chii tii kana kofi?	What do you want, tea or coffee?
Ndauya naamai.	I came with mother.
Ndasimuka kuti ndione.	I stood up so that I could see.
Aenda kuchipatara nekuti ari kurwara.	He/She went to the hospital because he/she is sick.

Tine musangano naizvozvo unofanira kuuya.	We have a meeting, so you should come.
Ndakamirira kudzimara ndaneta.	I waited until I got tired.
Akatanga kuenda kuchikoro kubvira January.	He/she has been going to school since January.
Ndakatanga kuziva Patricia kubvira muna 2000.	I have known Patricia since the year 2000.
Ndichaenda kutown uye ndichatenga bhuku.	I will go to town, and I will buy a book.
Ndinoda kuona Tino saka ndauya.	I want to see Tino; that is why I came.

Expressing Association with Personal Pronouns

na- + pronoun

na- + ini	neni	"with me"
na- + isu	nesu	"with us"
na- + iwe	newe	"with you" (*sg.*)
na- + imi	nemi	"with you" (*pl.* / *honorific*)
na- + iye	naye	"with him / her"
na- + ivo	navo	"with them"

Adverbs

An adverb serves to describe a verb in terms of degree, manner, time and place. Adverbs in Shona are both pure and derived. Derived adverbs are those that are derived from other grammatical categories; eg., verbs, adjectives, etc.

Expressing degree of frequency with ka-

When *ka-* is prefixed to a numerical adjective, it denotes the number of times.

kangani	how many times
kazhinji	many times
kashoma	few times
kamwe chete	once
kaviri	twice
katatu	three times

Akauya kangani?	How many times did he/she come?
Ndinodya bota kazhinji.	I eat porridge many times (often).
Ndinodya nyama kashoma.	I eat meat a few times (rarely).
Takauya kaviri.	We came twice.
Akapinda muchitoro katatu.	He went into the store three times.

Adverbs of manner

These are derived from verbs and adjectives.

zvinyoronyoro	softly	(adjective "nyoro" – soft, wet)
chinyararire	quietly	(verb "kunyarara" – to be quiet)

Adverbs of time

These do not differ from the noun form.

usiku	night
mangwana	tomorrow
nhasi	today
nezuro	yesterday

marimwezuro	the day before yesterday
gore	year
zuva	day

The use of **ne** gives repetitive or durational meaning to the following constructions when used adverbially.

siku nesikati	day and night
mwedzi nemwedzi	month after month
gore negore	year after year

Place

The locative nouns all function also as adverbs to denote location or place.

pasi	down, ground, floor
padyo	near
mberi	front
kure	far

EXERCISES

I. Complete the following sentences using the conjunction given in parentheses.

1. Unoda chii, tii _____ kofi? (or)
2. Ndabika chikafu _____ ndine nzara. (because)
3. _____ unogara kupi? (so)
4. Ndanwa tii _____ ndadya chingwa. (and)
5. Baba _____ amai vaenda kupi? (and)

II. Translate into English.

1. Gezai maoko.
2. ndipeiwo
3. Muchitendei.
4. Taguta.
5. Chikafu chiri kunaka.

III. Translate into Shona.

1. many times
2. sometimes
3. Thank you for calling.
4. few times
5. all times
6. How many times?
7. three times
8. once

IV. Practice and translate the following conversation.

1. Pamusoroi.
2. Gezai maoko.
3. Idyai chikafu.
4. Mazvita taguta.
5. Muchitendei.

LESSON
ELEVEN

DIALOGUE

Kubhanga

TELLER: Mangwanani.

LAURA: Mangwanani, marara sei?

TELLER: Ndarara, ndingakubatsirei nei?

LAURA: Ndiri kuda kuchinja maUS$. *Exchange rate* chii?

TELLER: I37.

LAURA: Zvakanaka. Oyi mari.

TELLER: Imarii yamuinayo?

LAURA: IUS$100.

TELLER: Zvakanaka, saka mari yenyu iZW$3700.

LAURA: Mazvita, ko hapana komisheni here?

TELLER: Kwete, hapana.

LAURA: Zvakanaka.

At the Bank

TELLER: Good morning.

LAURA: Good morning, how did you sleep?

TELLER: I slept well. How can I help you?

LAURA: I want to change US$. What is the exchange rate?

TELLER: It is 37.

LAURA: All right, here is the money.

TELLER: How much do you have?

LAURA: It is US$100.

TELLER: All right, so your money is ZW$3700.

LAURA: Thank you, is there no commission fee?

TELLER: No, there is not.

LAURA: All right.

VOCABULARY

chii?	what?
exchange rate	exchange rate
i37	it is 37
imarii	how much is it?
iUS$100	it is US$100
iZW$3700	it is ZW$3700
kubatsira	to help
kubhanga	at the bank
kuchinja	to change
kuda	to want
kurara	to sleep
mangwanani	good morning
mari	money
maUS$	US$
mazvita	thank you
ndiri	I am
nei?	with what?
oyi	here is
saka	so
sei?	how?
yamuinayo	that you have
yenyu	your
zvakanaka	all right

EXPRESSIONS

Mangwanani.	Good morning.
Marara sei?	How did you sleep?
Ndingakubatsire nei?	How can I help you?
Mazvita.	Thank you.
Imarii?	How much is it?

GRAMMAR

Object Pronouns

The object prefix (or pronoun) comes between the object and the verb. The object pronouns are:

me	**ndi-**	us	**ti-**
you	**ku-**	you (*pl.*)	**mu-**
him/her	**mu-**	them	**va-**
it	**chi-**	them ("it" *pl.*)	**zvi-**

EXAMPLES:

Akandirova pagumbo.	He hit me on the leg.
Takachirova.	We hit it.

Object Infixes for the Different Noun Categories

Noun Category	Object Infix
People	
sg. munhu "person"	**mu**
pl. vanhu "people"	**va**
Trees	
sg. muti "tree"	**u**
pl. miti "trees"	**i**
Hard-Sounding	
sg. banga "knife"	**ri**
pl. mapanga "knives"	**a**

Things
sg. chinhu "thing" **chi**
pl. zvinhu "things" **zvi**

Light-Sounding
sg. mombe "cow" **i**
pl. mombe "cows" **dzi**

Long Things
sg. ruoko "hand" **rwu**
pl. maoko "hands" **a**

Diminutive
sg. kasikana "little girl" **ka**
pl. twusikana "little girls" **twu**

Abstract
sg. upenyu "life" **hwu**

Verbal
sg. kudya "food, way of eating" **ku**

Locative
pamba "at the house" **pa**
kumba "to, from, towards the house" **ku**
mumba "in, inside the house" **mu**

Diminutive (*Karanga*)
svikomana "little boy" **svi**

Argumentative
sg. zirume "huge man" **ri**
pl. mazirume "huge men" **a**

Takavaona pamba.	We saw them at the house.
Vakachitenga kupi?	Where did they buy it?
Wakariona rinhi?	When did you see it?
Baba vakaiuraya nezuro.	Father slaughtered the cow yesterday.
Ndaritenga nhasi.	I bought it today. (the knife)

EXERCISES

I.   Give the diminutive forms for the following nouns.

1. mombe
2. musikana
3. miti
4. vana
5. bhazi

II. Translate.

1. I saw them (personal).
2. I saw it. (*sg.*)
3. I saw them ("it" *pl.*)
4. She saw me today.
5. They saw us yesterday.

III. Practice and translate the following conversation.

1. Mangawanani.
2. Marara sei?
3. Tarara mararawo.
4. Ndiri kuda mari.
5. Muri kuda marii?
6. Ndiri kuda ZW$1000.

LESSON
TWELVE

DIALOGUE

Kuchipatara

Nesi: Masikati amai, mwana akuvara sei?

Amai: Masikati nesi, mwana atsva gumbo.

Nesi: Atsva nei?

Amai: Atsva neaini.

Nesi: Imi manga muri kupi?

Amai: Ini ndanga ndiri kubasa.

Nesi: Ndichamuzora mushonga uyu, ndomusunga bhandeji. Ndichakupai mushonga wekunyaradza marwadzo. Haana kunyanya kukuvara.

Amai: Zvakanaka, ndatenda chaizvo.

Nesi: Munofanira kuuya nemwana kuti azorwe mushonga kwemasvondo maviri.

Amai: Zvakanaka, tichaonana mangwana.

At the Hospital

NURSE: Good afternoon mother, what happened to your child?

MOTHER: Good afternoon nurse, the child burned her leg.

NURSE: What burned her?

MOTHER: She was burned by an iron.

NURSE: Where were you?

MOTHER: I was at work.

NURSE: I will smear this medicine on her, then tie a bandage. I will give her a painkiller. She was not badly hurt.

MOTHER: All right, thank you very much.

NURSE: You are supposed to come with the child to have some medicine applied every day for two weeks.

MOTHER: All right, we will see each other tomorrow.

VOCABULARY

amai	mother
bhandeji	a bandage
chaizvo	very much
gumbo	leg
haana	she has not
imi	you
ini	I
kubasa	to work
kuchipatara	at the hospital
kufanira	to be supposed to
kukuvara	to be hurt
kunyanya	to be excessive
kunyaradza	to reduce/lessen (referring to the pain)
kuonana	to see each other
kupa	to give
kupi?	where?
kusunga	to tie
kutenda	to thank
kutsva	to be burned
kuuya	to come
kuvara	to be hurt
kuzoiswa	to be put
kuzora	to smear
kwemasvondo	for weeks
manga	you were
mangwana	tomorrow
marwadzo	pain
masikati	good afternoon
maviri	two
muri	you are

mushonga	medicine
mwana	child
ndanga	I was
ndiri	I am
neaini	by an iron
nei?	by what?
nemwana	with child
nesi	nurse
sei?	how?
uyu	this
zvakanaka	all right

EXPRESSION

Tichaonana.	We will see each other.

GRAMMAR

Verb Extensions

These are particular to Bantu languages in general; the extension expands the meaning of the verb. The verb extension occurs between the verb root and the terminal vowel "a".

The Passive Extension [-w-, -iw-, -ew-]

The passive is formed by adding the ending (infix) -w- to the verb root. When the verb root begins with a vowel, the alternative endings of the passive extension are -iw- or -ew-. The -iw- is used when the vowel of the verb root is **a**, **i**, or **u**. The -ew- is used when the vowel of the verbal root is **e** or **o**.

The passive indicates an action that has been done to or performed on the subject.

Verb root	Passive	
-tor-	*torwa*	be taken
-bik-	*bikwa*	be cooked
-tum-	*tumwa*	be sent
-chek-	*chekwa*	be cut

Ndatumwa naamai.   I have been sent by mother.
Mwana atorwa nababa.   The child has been taken by father.

The Neuter Extension [-ik-, -ek-]

The neuter verb suffix is -ik- when the final vowel of the verb root is **a**, **i**, or **u**, and -ek- when the final vowel of the verb root is **e** or **o**.

The neuter indicates actions that can be done easily.

roveka	easily beaten
oneka	visible
dyika	edible
nzwika	audible

Chikafu chinodyika   The food is edible.

The Causative Extension [-is-, -es-, -ts-, -dz-, -nz-]

This series of suffixes has the implication that an action has been made or caused to occur.

tyisa	cause to be afraid
endesa	cause to go
setsa	cause to laugh
fadza	cause to be happy
penza	cause to be crazy

The Benefactive Extension [-ir-, -er-]

The benefactive verb suffix is **-ir-** when the final vowel of the verb root is **a, i,** or **u**, and it is **-er-** when the final vowel of the verb root is **e** or **o**.

The benefactive signifies that the action is done to, for, or on behalf of someone.

nyora	*nyorera*	write to
bika	*bikira*	cook for
sevenza	*sevenzera*	work for
vaka	*vakira*	build for
tora	*torera*	take from

Amai vakabikira mwana.	Mother cooked for the child.
Musikana akatorera mwana mari.	The girl took money from the child.

The Reciprocal Extension [-an-]

The reciprocal suffix -an- indicates that the action is performed between two people, to each other.

uraya	*urayana*	kill each other
tuka	*tukana*	scold each other

Vakadzi vakatukana pachiteshi.	The women scolded each other at the station.

The Reflexive Extension [-zvi-]

The reflexive prefix indicates that an agent is performing an action on him/herself.

kuzviuraya	to kill oneself
kuzvishora	to blame oneself
kuzvitonga	to be independent.

Mukomana akazvitengera bhuku.	The boy bought himself a book.

EXERCISES

I. Give the benefactive form of the following verbs.

    1. bika
    2. taura
    3. mira
    4. nyora
    5. vaka
    6. sevenza

II. Identify the verb extensions.

    1. torwa
    2. kuzvishora
    3. nwika
    4. onana
    5. endesa
    6. tambira

III. Translate.

    1. We will see each other tomorrow.
    2. Come tomorrow.
    3. to get burned
    4. to smear
    5. two weeks

IV. Practice and translate the following conversation.

    1. Masikati nesi.
    2. Masikati amai, maswera sei?
    3. Ndaswera maswerawo.

4. Taswera.
5. Ndingakubatsirei nei amai?
6. Mwana atsva gumbo neaini.
7. Zvakanaka, ndichamuzora mushonga.
8. Ndatenda.

KEY TO
EXERCISES

Lesson One

I.

1. Handisi kudya.
2. Tendai haadzidzi ChiShona.
3. Havaendi.
4. Hausi kudya.
5. Hatidzidzi History.

II.

1. Wakadini/Makadini?
2. Unogara kupi?
3. Unodzidza chii?
4. Masikati.
5. Mhoro(i).
6. Shamwari yangu.
7. Ndafara kukuziva.
8. Ndinonzi Tendai.
9. Zvakanaka.
10. Waswera sei?/Maswera sei?

III.

1. Ndinodzidza Shona.
2. Vanodya chingwa.
3. Munobva kuAmerica.
4. Tinoenda kuZimbabwe.
5. Anoenda kuUniversity.

IV.

1. Ndi-
2. Ti-
3. U-
4. Mu-
5. A-
6. Va-

V.

1. Good afternoon.
2. How did you spend the day?
3. We spent the day well, what about you?
4. Where do your parents live?
5. What do you study at the University?
6. I am happy to know you.

Lesson Two

I.

1. Ndiri muAmerican.
2. Tiri vadzidzi?
3. Mabhazi anowanikwa kupi?
4. Kune mhepo here?
5. Ndinotaura Shona.

II.

1. Ndingabvunzewo here?
2. Hongu.
3. Bvunzai zvenyu.
4. Ndatenda chaizvo.
5. Zvakanaka.
6. Muchitendei.

III.

1. usafambe
2. usataure
3. usadzidze
4. usatenge
5. usafare
6. usasevenze
7. usaende

IV.

Verb	Imperative Singular	Imperative Plural
bvunza	bvunza	bvunzai
taura	taura	taurai
-dya	idya	idyai
famba	famba	fambai
mira	mira	mirai

V.

1. Excuse me, do you speak Shona?
2. Yes, I speak Shona.
3. Where can I get buses that go to Zengeza?
4. At the Charge Office.
5. Thank you.
6. All right.

Lesson Three

I.

1. Handina kufamba.
2. Havana kuenda.
3. Hataidzidza.

4. Hauna kunwa.
5. Haana kudya.

II.

1. Masikati.
2. Ndingakubatsirei nei?
3. Maswera sei?

4. Tichaonana.
5. Ndipei mari.

III.

1. Ndichaenda.
2. Achaenda.
3. Vachadzidza.

4. Uchanwa.
5. Muchataura.

IV.

1. Nda-
2. Ta-
3. Wa-

4. Ma-
5. A-
6. Va-

V.

1. Good afternoon.
2. Good afternoon.
3. How did you spend the day?
4. I spent the day well, how about you?
5. I spent the day well.
6. How can I help you?
7. I want to get a passport.
8. All right.

Lesson Four

I.

1. ida/idai
2. rara/rarai
3. swera/swerai
4. gara/garai
5. batsira/batsirai
6. bvunza/bvunzai

II.

1. Nhasi chingani?
2. Mangwana Chipiri.
3. Une makore mangani?
4. Nhasi Chitatu.
5. Nhasi dheti chii?

III.

1. Good evening.
2. Good evening.
3. I want a room for the night.
4. All right, how many are you?
5. We are two. How much does it cost?
6. It's ZW$1520.
7. Thank you.

Lesson Five

I.

1. vasikana
2. vana
3. mapanga
4. mazai
5. vanhu
6. tsamba
7. tukomana
8. upenyu
9. zvikwama
10. urombo

II.

1. Banga riri kupi?
2. Mapanga ari kupi?
3. Tsamba iri kupi? (sg.)
4. Tsamba dziri kupi? (pl.)
5. Kasikana kari kupi?
6. Tusikana twuri/turi kupi?

III.

1. Chisarai
2. Kudhura
3. Ndipeiwo
4. Imarii?
5. Tava kuenda.

IV.

1. Excuse me.
2. How can I help you?
3. I want to buy bananas and vegetebles.
4. It costs ZW$500.
5. Give me some vegetables.
6. All right.

Lesson Six

I.

1. Mazai angu.
2. Mwana wenyu.
3. Kamwana kake.
4. Upenyu hwavo.
5. Zvinhu zvedu.
6. Bhuku rako.
7. Mumba mavo.
8. Upenyu hwake.
9. Pikicha yangu.
10. Zvipo zvako.

II.

1. mwana wangu
2. Pinda mumba mangu.
3. kasikana kake
4. Tiri kuenda kuchikoro kwedu.
5. Tiri kubva kuchikoro kwavo.

III.

1. Good afternoon, where do you want to go?
2. I want to go to the University.
3. All right.
4. How much is it to get to the University?

5. It's only ZW$200.
6. Here is ZW$200.
7. Thank you, go well.

Lesson Seven

I.

1. Mwana uyu achaenda. (this)
2. Bhazi iro rava kuenda. (that)
3. Musikana uyo auya rinhi? (that)
4. Ndinoda hembe iyi. (this)
5. Vakomana ava vanogara naani? (these)

II.

1. Nyika yose.
2. Munhu murefu refu.
3. Vanhu avo.
4. (Ini) ndega.
5. Vanhu vazhinji.

III.

1. Ndakauya ndega.
2. Iye womene akaenda.
3. Vanhu vose vakadya.
4. mazuva mashomashoma
5. musikana mupfupi

IV.

1. Knock, knock. May we come in?
2. You may come in. Enter. Sit down.
3. Hello.
4. Hello. How are you?
5. We are fine, what about you?
6. We are fine.
7. How are others?
8. They are fine.

Lesson Eight

I.

1. Zvakanaka.
2. Ndeipi?
3. Ndiri raiti.

4. Achiri kudya.
5. Ndingauyewo here?

II.

1. Tingadyewo here?

2. Tichiri kudya.

III.

1. Ndingabvunzewo?
2. Ndingagarewo?
3. Ndingataurewo?

4. Ndingabatsirewo?
5. Ndingaendewo?

IV.

1. Hello, Tendai, what's up?
2. Nothing special.
3. I want to invite you to a party.
4. All right friend, when?
5. On Thursday.
6. What time is the party?
7. It starts at 6:30 in the evening.
8. All right, I will come.
9. Thank you.

Lesson Nine

I.

1. Imarii?
2. Inguvai?
3. Waenda sei?

4. Une makore mangani?
5. Wakauya rinhi?

II.

1. Unotaura Shona <u>here</u>?
2. Unonzi <u>ani</u>?
3. Tichaenda kuchikoro <u>rinhi</u>?
4. Makarara <u>nguvai</u>?
5. Vanogara <u>kupi</u>?

III.

1. Excuse me, we want to buy a book.
2. What is the title of the book?
3. It is called *History of Zimbabwe*.
4. I am sorry, we do not have it.
5. All right, thank you very much.

Lesson Ten

I.

1. Unoda chii, tii <u>kana</u> kofi? (or)
2. Ndabika chikafu <u>nekuti</u> ndine nzara. (because)
3. <u>Saka</u> unogara kupi? (so)
4. Ndanwa tii <u>uye</u> ndadya chingwa. (and)
5. Baba <u>na</u>amai vaenda kupi? (and)

II.

1. Wash your hands.
2. give me
3. You are welcome.
4. We are full.
5. The food is good.

III.

1. kazhinji
2. dzimwe nguva
3. Ndatenda nekufona.
4. kashoma
5. nguva dzose
6. Kangani?
7. katatu
8. kamwe chete

IV.

1. Excuse me.
2. Wash your hands.
3. Eat the food.

4. Thank you, we are full.
5. You are welcome.

Lesson Eleven

I.

1. kamombe.
2. kamusikana.
3. tumiti.

4. tuvana.
5. kabhazi

II.

1. Ndavaona.
2. Ndachiona
3. Ndazviona.

4. Andiona nhasi.
5. Vakationa nezuro.

III.

1. Good morning.
2. How did you sleep?
3. We slept well, how about you?
4. I want money.
5. How much money do you want?
6. I want ZW$1000.

Lesson Twelve

I.

1. bikira.
2. taurira.
3. mirira.

4. nyorera.
5. vakira.
6. sevenzera.

II.

1. passive.
2. reflexive.
3. neuter.

4. reciprocal.
5. causative.
6. benefactive.

III.

1. Tichaonana mangwana.
2. Uya mangwana.
3. kutsva

4. kuzora
5. masvondo maviri

IV.

1. Good afternoon, nurse.
2. Good afternoon, mother, how did you spend the day?
3. I spent it well, how about you?
4. I spent it well.
5. How can I help you, mother?
6. The child got burned on the leg by an iron.
7. All right, I will smear on some medicine.
8. Thank you.

VOCABULARY

SHONA-ENGLISH VOCABULARY

A

abika she cooked
aita he/she did
amai mother
ane he/she has
ani who
ano these
anoenda that go
anokwirirwa they are boarded
anowanikwa they are found
asi but
atsva he/she burned

B

baba father
banga knife
batsira help
bhandeji bandage
bhazi bus
bho-o good (slang, informal)
bhuku book
bveni baboon
bvunza ask (imperative)
bvunzai you may ask

C

chaizvo very much
chamhembe north
chando cold
cheka cut
chena white
chenji change
chete only
chii what
chikafu food
chikoro school
Chikumi June
Chikunguru July
chikwama wallet
China Thursday
chingwa bread
chinhu thing
Chipiri Tuesday
chipo gift
chiri it is
chirimo warm dry season
chisarai goodbye
Chishanu Friday
Chitatu Wednesday
chitoro store
Chivabvu May
chokwadi truth

D

dada be proud
dare court
dhadha duck
dheti date
dhongi donkey
diki small
doro beer
dzimba animal footprint
dziri that is

E

edzai try
enda go

F

famba walk, travel

G

gara sit/stay/live
garai sit
gezai wash
gogoi knock, knock
gore year
gudo baboon
gumbo leg
gumi ten
Gumiguru October

Gunyana September
guta to be full

H

haana she has not
hama relative/s
hatina we do not have
hatizivi we do not know
hembe dress
here interrogative marker
hesi hi
hombe big
hongu yes
ho-o is it?
horaiti all right

I

ibva be ripe
ichaitwa it will be held
idyai eat
imarii how much is it?
imba house (LT)
imba sing (HT)
imbwa dog
imi you (pl.)
ina four
ini I
inotora it takes
inwa drink
inwai (you) drink
ipati it is a party

iri it is
isu we
ivo they
iwe you (sg.)
iye he, she
izwi word, voice

J

jamu jam
jira cloth

K

kakomana little/small boy
kamwana small child
kamwe once
kana if/or, when, even
kasikana little/small girl
katsi cat
ko so, what about
kobvu fat
kora collar
kubasa to work
kubhanga at the bank
kubika to cook
kubva to come from
kubvira since
Kubvumbi April
kuchema to cry
kuchikoro to school
kuchinja to change
kuchipatara to the hospital

kuda to want; to love, like
kudakara until
kudhura to be expensive
kudya food
kudya to eat
kudzidza to learn, study
kudzimara until
kuenda to go
kufamba to travel
kugara to stay, live, sit
kugona to be able
Kukadzi February
kukoka to invite
kukukoka to invite you
kukuvara to be hurt
kumba to the house
kunaka to taste good/to be beautiful
kunetsa to be a problem
kunwa to drink
kunyanya to be a lot
kunyarara to be quiet
kupasa to pass
kupati to a party
kupi where
kuri it is
kurova to beat
kuru big
Kurume March
kurwadza to be painful
kuseka to laugh
kusvikako to get there
kutamba to play, dance
kutambira to receive
kutaura to speak

kutenda to thank
kutenga to buy
kuti to say, that
kutora to take
kutsvaga to look for
kuuya to come
kuzoiswa to be put
kuzvarwa to be born
kwakadii how is it?
kwamabva where are you from?
kwanga it was
kwava it is now
kwawaita that you did
kwemanheru of evening
kwemasvondo for weeks

M

mabhanana bananas
mabhazi buses
mabvazuva east
machira cloths
madokero west
makadini how are you?
makadiniwo how are you (also)?
makore clouds
makudo baboons
manga you were
mangani how many
mangwana tomorrow
mangwanani good morning
manheru good evening
maodzanyemba south
maoko hands

maorenji oranges
mapanga knives
marara you slept
mari money
marimwezuro the day before yesterday
marwadzo pain
masikati good afternoon
maswera you spent the day
maswerawo you spent the day also
matare courts
matatu three
maviri two
mazai eggs
mazuva days
mazvita thank you
mberi front
Mbudzi November
mheni lightning
mhepo wind
mhoroi hello
mhuri family
mira stop
miti trees
miuyu baobabs
mombe cow
mubvunzo question
muchagara you will stay
muchitendei you are welcome
Mugovera Saturday
mukomana boy
muna along
mune you have

munhu person
munoda you want
munofanira you are supposed
muri you are
muriwo vegetables
murumu in room
musanetseke you do not bother
mushonga medicine
musi day
musikana girl
musoro head
mutengesi seller
muti tree
mutyairi driver
muuyu baobab tree
Muvhuro Monday
mvura water, rain
mwaka season
mwana child
mwanangu my child
mwedzi moon, month

N

naani by whom
naka be sweet, beautiful
nama seal
ndanga I was
ndarara I slept
ndarasika I am lost
ndaswera I spent the day well
ndatenda thank you
ndava I am about
ndega I alone

ndeipi what's up?
ndiani who
ndiburutsei drop me
ndichaedza I will try
ndichakupai I will give you
ndichamuzora I will smear on her
ndichasvika I will arrive
ndidzo is the one
ndikubikirei cook for you
ndine I have
ndingabvunzawo may I ask
ndingakubatsire can I help you
ndinoda I want
ndipe give me
ndipeiwo give me (polite)
Ndira January
ndiri I am
nditsvage I look
ndiyoyo it is
ndomusunga then I tie her
neaini by iron
nebhangi the bank
nechii and what
nei with what
nekufona for phoning
nekuti because
nemaapuro and apples
nemuriwo and vegetables
nemwana with child
nesi nurse
nezuro yesterday
ngani how many
ngano folktale
nguva time

ngwara be clever
nhai is it
nhasi today
nhau news
nomwe seven
nyama meat
Nyamavhuvhu August
nyika country
nyora write
nyota thirst
nzara hunger (LT)
nzara fingernail (HT)
nzou elephant

O

okeyi okay
ona see
oyi /oi here is

P

paCharge Office at the Charge Office
padyo near
pamhi broad
pamusoroi excuse me
pano here
papi (at) where
pasi down
pasi floor, ground
pasipoti passport
patafura at the table
pfumbu gray

pfumbamwe nine
pfupi short
pikicha picture
pindai enter
piri two
poshi one

R

raiti right/ok/fine
rakanyorwa it was written
rara sleep
refu tall, long
regai let me
rimwe one
rinhi when
rinonzi that is called
rize scorpion
rufaro happiness
rugare peace
ruoko hand
ruvengo hatred
rwizi river

S

sadza sadza [staple food in Zimbabwe]
saka so
sango forest
sarudza choose
sei how
sere eight

sevenza work
shamwari friend
shanda work
shanu five
shava brown
shoma few
shora blame (HT)
shora yellow (LT)
shumba lion
svika enter
svikai you may enter
Svondo Sunday

T

taguta we are full
tanhatu six
taswera we spent the day well
tatenda thank you
tatu three
taura speak
tema black
tete thin (LT)
tichaonana we will see each other
tiende we go
tii tea
tingabvunzewo may we ask
tingariwane we can get it
tiri we are
tiripo we are fine
tisvikewo may we enter
torai take
tsamba letter

tsvuku red
tuka scold
tukomana little/small boys
tuma send
tusikana little girls
twana little/small children
tyora break

U

udzoke you come back
upenyu life
upfumi wealth
uraya kill
uri you are
urombo poverty
usiku evening
uya come
uyai come (pl.)
uye and
uyo that
uyu this

V

vadzidzi students
vaeni visitors
vaka build
vakadii how are they
vakadzi women
vakomana boys
vamwe others
vana children

vangani how many
vanhu people
varipo they are fine
vasikana girls
vava be sour
vhara close
visa visa

W

waita you did
wangu my
waswera did you spend the
   day well?
wava you are now
wazvita thank you
weChishanu on Friday
wekunyaradza to lessen
wenyu your
wotoshingirira you have to
   persevere

Y

yacho that particular one
yadhi yard
yako your (sg.)

yamuinayo that which you have
yei for what
yekunwa to drink
yekurara to sleep
yenyu your

Z

zai egg
zhinji many
zhizha summer
zino tooth
zuva day, sun
zvakanaka all right
zvako you (sg.) yourself
zvanzi it was said
zvavo they themselves
zvedu we ourselves
zvenyu you (pl.) yourselves
zvikoro schools
zvikwama wallets
zvingwa bread (pl.)
zvinhu things
zvino now
zvipo gifts
zviri they are
Zvita December
zvitoro stores

REFERENCES

Beach, D. *The Shona and Their Neighbours.* Oxford: Basil Blackwell,1994.

Beckett, C. and Koreka, S. *A Pocket Guide to Zimbabwe.* Harare: Mond Books, 1999.

Brauner, S. *A Grammatical Sketch of Shona.* Koln: Koppe, 1995.

Cerna, I. and Machalek, J. *Beginner's Czech.* New York: Hippocrene Books, 1994.

Chimhundu, H. and Mashiri, P. *Taurai ChiShona.* Zimbabwe: Juta, 1996.

Chitauro, M. et al. "Song, Story and Nation: Women as singers and actresses in Zimbabwe" In *Politics and Performance: Theatre, Poetry and Song in Southern Africa.* Johannesburg: University of Witwatersrand Press, 1994.

Dale, D. *Shona Companion.* Gweru: Mambo Press, 1968.

Inter-Censal Demographic Survey Report, Harare: Zimbabwe, 1997.

Mashiri, P. 2001. *Beyond Categorial Boundaries: An Outline of Derived Adjectives in Shona.* Unpublished Paper. Department of African Languages & Literature. University of Zimbabwe.

Mawadza, A. *Shona-English/English-Shona Dictionary and Phrasebook: A Language of Zimbabwe.* New York: Hippocrene Books, 2000.

Ruzhowa, D. *Learning Shona.* Harare: Harper Collins Publishers, 1997.

African Language Titles from Hippocrene...

Shona-English/English-Shona Dictionary & Phrasebook
1,400 entries • 174 pages • 3¾ x 7½ • ISBN 0-7818-0813-8 •
$11.95pb • (167)

Afrikaans-English/English-Afrikaans Practical Dictionary, Revised
25,000 entries • 430 pages • 5 x 7 • ISBN 0-7818-0846-4 •
$17.95pb • (243)

Bemba-English/English-Bemba Concise Dictionary
10,000 entries • 233 pages • 4 x 6 • ISBN 0-7818-0630-5 •
$13.95pb • (709)

Fulani-English Practical Dictionary
10,000 entries • 242 pages • 5 x 7¼ • ISBN 0-7818-0404-3 •
$14.95pb • (38)

Hausa-English/English-Hausa Practical Dictionary
18,000 entries • 431 pages • 5 x 7 • ISBN 0-7818-0426-4 •
$16.95pb • (499)

Igbo-English/English-Igbo Dictionary & Phrasebook
1,400 entries • 186 pages • 3¾ x 7½ • ISBN 0-7818-0661-5 •
$11.95pb • (750)

Malagasy-English/English-Malagasy Dictionary & Phrasebook
2,500 entries • 170 pages • 3¾ x 7½ • ISBN 0-7818-0843-X •
$11.95pb • (256)

Pulaar-English/English-Pulaar Standard Dictionary
30,000 entries • 276 pages • 5½ x 8½ • ISBN 0-7818-0479-5 •
$19.95pb • (600)

Somali-English/English-Somali Dictionary & Phrasebook
3,500 entries • 176 pages • 3¾ x 7½ • ISBN 0-7818-0621-6 •
$13.95pb • (755)

Swahili-English/English-Swahili Dictionary & Phrasebook
5,000 entries • 200 pages • 3¾ x 7½ • ISBN 0-7818-0905-3 •
$11.95pb • (231)

Swahili-English/English-Swahili Practical Dictionary
35,000 entries • 600 pages • 4½ x 7 • ISBN 0-7818-0480-9 •
$19.95pb • (606)

Twi-English/English-Twi Concise Dictionary
6,000 entries • 332 pages • 4 x 6 • ISBN 0-7818-0264-4 •
$12.95pb • (290)

Yoruba-English/English-Yoruba Modern Practical Dictionary
30,000 entries • 500 pages • 5½ x 8½ • ISBN 0-7818-0978-9 •
$19.95pb • (471)

Other African Interest Titles

Treasury of African Love Poems and Proverbs

A selection of songs and sayings from numerous African languages—including Swahili, Yoruba, Berber, Zulu and Amharic.

128 pages • 5 x 7 • ISBN 0-7818-0483-3 • $11.95hc • (611)

African Proverbs

This collection of 1,755 proverbs spans all regions of the African continent. They are arranged alphabetically by key words. Charmingly illustrated throughout.

135 pages • 6 x 9 • 20 illustrations • ISBN 0-7818-0691-7 •
$17.50hc • (778)

African Cookbooks

Best of Regional African Cooking
274 pages • 5½ x 8½ • ISBN 0-7818-0598-8 • $11.95pb • (684)

Traditional South African Cookery
178 pages • 5 x 8½ • ISBN 0-7818-0490-6 • $10.95pb • (352)

All prices subject to change without prior notice. **To purchase Hippocrene Books** contact your local bookstore, call (718) 454-2366, visit www.hippocrenebooks.com, or write to: Hippocrene Books, 171 Madison Avenue, New York, NY 10016. Please enclose check or money order, adding $5.00 shipping (UPS) for the first book and $.50 for each additional book.